# Learn Python in On

## (Second Edition)

# --Workbook--

By Jamie Chan
https://www.learncodingfast.com/python

Copyright © 2019

# Preface

This book is designed to be the accompanying workbook for the book "Learn Python In One Day and Learn It Well (2nd Edition)" by the same author.

If you are new to Python, you are strongly encouraged to get the above-mentioned book and use this accompanying workbook to help you in your learning.

If you are familiar with Python, you can use this book as a standalone workbook to test and improve your knowledge of the Python syntax, or use it as a compilation of examples, providing you with a quick reference to the syntax.

The goal of this workbook is to help you build your programming skills one concept at a time before working on bigger projects.

At the end of the book, there are two projects for you to work on to help you consolidate your learning and see how it all works together.

You can download the source code for the questions, solutions and projects at
https://www.learncodingfast.com/python

Any errata can be found at
https://www.learncodingfast.com/errata

## Contact Information

I would love to hear from you.
For feedback or queries, you can contact me at
jamie@learncodingfast.com.

## More Books by Jamie

Python: Learn Python in One Day and Learn It Well (1st Edition)

Python: Learn Python in One Day and Learn It Well (2nd Edition)

C#: Learn C# in One Day and Learn It Well

Java: Learn Java in One Day and Learn It Well

CSS: Learn CSS in One Day and Learn It Well

SQL: Learn SQL (using MySQL) in One Day and Learn It Well

# Table of Contents

# Chapter 1: Introduction

Thank you for picking up this book.

This book is designed to be a workbook for the book "Learn Python In One Day and Learn It Well (2nd Edition)" by the same author. It can also be used as a standalone workbook for you to test and improve your knowledge of the Python syntax.

Each question in this workbook is designed to test one or two key concepts. All solutions are extensively tested by a group of beta readers. The solutions provided are simplified as much as possible so that they can serve as examples for you to refer to when you are learning a new syntax.

Once you are familiar with the concepts tested in different chapters, you can work on the two projects at the end of the book to help you consolidate your learning. These projects require the application of topics covered in previous chapters and allow you to see how everything works together.

A few advanced concepts (like recursion and abstract methods) that were not covered in the main book will also be covered and explained in this book when we go through the projects.

### Formatting Guidelines

The book uses the following formatting guidelines:

Python code, variable names, values to be assigned, parameters and arguments will be presented in `Monospaced` font.

Output that you are required to display on the screen will be presented in *italics* in the question section.

User input is presented in ***italics bold***.

File names will be *underlined and presented in italics*.

## *Suggested Solutions*

Note that the answers provided in this book are only suggested solutions. Your solution may differ. As long as your solution behaves as described in the question, chances are your solution is valid too. The desired outputs for all questions are provided where applicable, either in the question or answer section.

The answers can be found at the end of each chapter. Some of the code consists of rather long statements. Hence, some statements may wrap around to the next line, making them difficult to read.

If you have a problem reading the code, you can download the source code for the questions, solutions and projects at https://www.learncodingfast.com/python.

*Note that this workbook is designed for beginners. If you are an advanced programmer, this workbook will likely not be as useful.*

# Chapter 2: Getting Ready for Python

## *Integrated Development Environment*

Before we start coding in Python, we need to install an integrated development environment.

Python code resembles the English language which computers are unable to understand. Code that we write in Python has to be "translated" into a language that computers can understand. This is done using a special program known as the Python interpreter.

An integrated development environment (IDE) is a software application that includes an editor for you to type your code and an interpreter to translate the code. We can also use the IDE to run our code and view the output.

## *Installing an IDE on your computer*

If you have yet to install any Python IDE on your computer, you can download a free IDE called IDLE.

Please go over to https://learncodingfast.com/how-to-install-python/ for detailed instructions on how to install and use IDLE.

Instructions are available on the accompanying site of this workbook so that whenever there are any changes to the IDE, you can find the updated instructions on the site. This will ensure that you'll always get the latest installation instructions.

Note that this book uses Python 3. Hence, you will have to run the code using an IDE that runs on Python 3 (preferably 3.4 and above). If you use Python 2, some of the code will not run properly.

Subsequent chapters consist mainly of questions and solutions, with discussions of the solutions where applicable. If you are asked to write some code, you are strongly encouraged to write the code inside the IDE and execute your code to see if it produces the desired output.

Ready to start? Let's go!

# Chapter 3: The World of Variables and Operators

### Question 1

Assign the number 11 to a variable called myFavNumber.

### Question 2

Assign the string 'Python' to a variable called myFavWord.

### Question 3

Assign the string 'Lee' to a variable called userName and use the print() function to print the value of userName.

After printing the value of userName, update userName to 'James' and print it again.

Note: The print() function is a built-in Python function that we use to display messages, values of variables or results of mathematical operations.

We simply enclose the message, variable name or mathematical expression inside the pair of parentheses. For instance, to print the value of userName, we write

```
print(userName)
```

### Question 4

Determine the output of the following program without running the code:

```
num1 = 5
NUM1 = 7

print(num1)
```

```
print(NUM1)
```

## Question 5

Explain what is wrong with the following statement:

```
1num = 7 + 5
```

## Question 6

Determine the output of the following program without running the code:

```
a = 17
b = 12
a = b
print(a)
```

## Question 7

Determine the output of the following program without running the code:

```
x, y = 5, 4

print(x+y)
print(x-y)
print(x*y)
print(x/y)
print(x//y)
print(x%y)
print(x**y)
```

## Question 8

Assign the values 12 and 5 to two variables a and b respectively.

Find the sum and product of a and b and assign the results to another two variables called sum and product respectively.

Find the remainder when a is divided by b and assign the result to a variable called `remainder`.

Print the values of `sum`, `product` and `remainder`.

## Question 9

Assign the values 13, 7 and 5 to three variables a, b and c respectively. Use the variables to evaluate the mathematical expression below:

```
(13 + 5)*7 + 5 - 13
```

Assign the result to a variable called `result` and print the value of `result`.

## Question 10

Determine the output of the following program without running the code:

```
s = 12
s = s - 3
print(s)
```

## Question 11

Assign the value 5 to a variable called `num`. Next, add 10 to `num` and assign the result back to `num`. Print the value of `num`.

## Question 12

Determine the output of the following program without running the code:

```
t = 10
t = t + 1
t = t*2
t = t/5
print(t)
```

# Question 13

Determine the output of the following program without running the code:

```
p, q = 12, 4

p += 3
print(p)

q **= 2
print(q)
```

# Question 14

Assign the values 11 and 7 to two variables r and s respectively. Add r to s and assign the result back to r. Print the values of r and s.

# Question 15

Think of an integer and assign it to a variable. Perform the following steps on the variable:

Add 17 to it.
Double the result.
Subtract 4 from the result.
Double the result again.
Add 20 to the result.
Divide the result by 4.
Subtract 20 from the result.

Each step involves operating on the result from the previous step and assigning the new result back to the variable.

Print the final answer. What number do you get?

## *Chapter 3: Answers*

### Question 1

```
myFavNumber = 11
```

### Question 2

```
myFavWord = 'Python'
```

### Question 3

```
userName = 'Lee'
print(userName)
userName = 'James'
print(userName)
```

Output

Lee
James

### Question 4

5
7

### Question 5

Variable names cannot start with a number. Hence, the name `1num` is not allowed as it starts with the number 1.

### Question 6

12

### Question 7

9

1
20
1.25
1
1
625

## Question 8

```
a = 12
b = 5

sum = a + b
product = a*b
remainder = a%b

print(sum)
print(product)
print(remainder)
```

## Output

17
60
2

## Question 9

```
a = 13
b = 7
c = 5

result = (a+c)*b + c - a
print(result)
```

## Output

118

# Question 10

9

# Question 11

```
num = 5
num = num + 10
print(num)
```

Output

15

# Question 12

4.4

# Question 13

15
16

# Question 14

```
r = 11
s = 7
r = r + s
print(r)
print(s)
```

Output

18
7

# Question 15

```
number = 10
number = number + 17
```

```
number = number*2
number = number - 4
number = number*2
number = number + 20
number = number/4
number = number - 20

print(number)
```

## Output

10.0

Note: You will get back the original number, converted to a decimal number due to the division.

# Chapter 4: Data Types in Python

## Question 1

Determine the output of the following program without running the code:

```
name1 = 'Jamie'
print(name1)

name2 = 'Aaron'.upper()
print(name2)

message = 'The names are %s and %s.' %(name1, name2)
print(message)
```

## Question 2

Assign the strings `'Python'`, `'Java'` and `'C#'` to three variables `lang1`, `lang2` and `lang3` respectively.

Use the three variables and the `%` operator to generate the following strings:

*The most popular programming languages are Python, Java and C#.*

*The most popular programming languages are Python, C# and Java.*

Assign the new strings to `message1` and `message2` respectively and print the values of `message1` and `message2`.

## Question 3

Determine the output of the following program without running the code:

```
num = 12
```

```
message = '%d' % (num)
print(message)

message = '%4d' % (num)
print(message)
```

## Question 4

Determine the output of the following program without running the code:

```
decnum = 1.72498329745

message = '%5.3f' % (decnum)
print(message)

message = '%7.2f' % (decnum)
print(message)
```

## Question 5

Assign the values 111 and 13 to two variables p and q respectively.

Divide p by q and assign the result to a variable called result.

Use the three variables and the % operator to generate the following string:

*The result of 111 divided by 13 is 8.538, correct to 3 decimal places.*

Assign the string to a variable called message and print the value of message.

## Question 6

Determine the output of the following program without running the code:

```
message = 'My name is {} and I am {} years
old.'.format('Jamie', 31)
print(message)
```

## Question 7

Determine the output of the following program without running the code:

```
message1 = 'My favorite colors are {}, {} and
{}.'.format('orange', 'blue', 'black')

message2 = 'My favorite colors are {1}, {0} and
{2}.'.format('orange', 'blue', 'black')

print(message1)
print(message2)
```

## Question 8

Assign the strings 'Aaron', 'Beck' and 'Carol' to three variables student1, student2 and student3 respectively.

Use the three variables and the format() method to generate the following string:

*My best friends are Aaron, Beck and Carol.*

Assign the new string to a variable called message and print the value of message.

## Question 9

Determine the output of the following program without running the code:

```
message1 = '{:7.2f} and {:d}'.format(21.3124, 12)

message2 = '{1} and {0}'.format(21.3124, 12)
```

```
print(message1)
print(message2)
```

## Question 10

Assign the values 12 and 7 to two variables x and y respectively.

Divide x by y and assign the result to a variable called quotient.

Use the format() method and the variables x, y and quotient to generate the following string:

*The result of 12 divided by 7 is 1.7143, correct to 4 decimal places.*

Assign the string to a variable called message and print the value of message.

## Question 11

Assign the value 2.7123 to a variable called number. Cast number into an integer and assign it back to number. Print the value of number.

## Question 12

How do you convert the number 2.12431 into a string?

## Question 13

Assign the string '12' to a variable called userInput. Cast userInput into an integer and assign it back to userInput. Print the value of userInput.

## Question 14

Given that myList = [1, 2, 3, 4, 5, 6], what is the number at index 1 and index -2? Explain why index 6 is invalid.

## Question 15

Assign the numbers 10, 11, 12 and 13 to a list called testScores.

Print the numbers at index 3 and index -1.

## Question 16

Determine the output of the following program without running the code:

```
myList = [1, 2, 3, 4, 5, 6, 7, 8, 9, 10]
myList1 = myList
myList2 = myList[3:6]
myList3 = myList[:5]
myList4 = myList[2:]
myList5 = myList[1:7:2]
myList6 = myList[ : :3]

print(myList)
print(myList1)
print(myList2)
print(myList3)
print(myList4)
print(myList5)
print(myList6)
```

## Question 17

Assign the values 11, 12, 13, 14, 15, 16, 17, 18, 19 and 20 to a list called q17.

Use a slice to select the numbers 13 to 18 from q17 and assign them to a new list called sliceA.

Use another slice to select the numbers 13, 16 and 19 from q17 and assign them to a list called sliceB.

Use the print() function to print sliceA and sliceB.

## Question 18

Create a list called `emptyList` with no initial values.
Add the numbers 12, 5, 9 and 11 to `emptyList` and use the
`print()` function to print the list.

## Question 19

Assign the numbers 1, 2, 3, 4 and 5 to a list called `q19`.

Next, change the third number to 10 and use the `print()`
function to print the list.

## Question 20

Assign the letters `'A'`, `'B'`, `'C'`, `'D'` and `'E'` to a list called `q20`.

Remove `'A'` and `'C'` from the list and print the list.

Hint: It is easier to remove `'C'` first. Why do you think that is so?

## Question 21

Assign the strings `'Sun'`, `'Mon'`, `'Tues'`, `'Wed'`, `'Thurs'`, `'Fri'`
and `'Sat'` to a tuple called `daysOfWeek`.

Assign the third element in `daysOfWeek` to a variable called
`myDay` and print the value of `myDay`.

## Question 22

What is wrong with the following dictionary?

```
nameAgeDict = {'John':12, 'Matthew':15, 'Aaron':13,
'John':14, 'Melvin':10}
```

## Question 23

Determine the output of the following program without running the code:

```
dict1 = {'Aaron': 11, 'Betty': 5, 0: 'Zero', 3.9:
'Three'}

print(dict1['Aaron'])
print(dict1[0])
print(dict1[3.9])

dict1['Aaron'] = 12
print(dict1)

del dict1['Betty']
print(dict1)
```

## Question 24

The statement below shows one way of declaring and initializing a dictionary called dict1.

```
dict1 = {'One':1, 'Two':2, 'Three':3, 'Four':4,
'Five':5}
```

(a) **Rewrite** the statement above using the dict() method to declare and initialize dict1.

(b) Print the item with key = 'Four'.

(c) Modify the item with key = 'Three'. Change it from 3 to 3.1.

(d) Delete the item with key = 'Two'.

(e) Use the print() function to print dict1.

## Question 25

Create a dictionary that maps the following countries to their respective capitals. The capitals are indicated in parenthesis beside the country names below.

USA (Washington, D.C.)
United Kingdom (London)
China (Beijing)
Japan (Tokyo)
France (Paris)

The country name should serve as the key for accessing the capital.

Next, print the dictionary.

Delete the third country from the dictionary and print it again.

Add the following two countries to the dictionary and print it again.

Germany (Berlin)
Malaysia (Kuala Lumpur)

---

## Chapter 4: Answers

### Question 1

Jamie
AARON
The names are Jamie and AARON.

### Question 2

```
lang1 = 'Python'
lang2 = 'Java'
lang3 = 'C#'

message1 = 'The most popular programming languages
are %s, %s and %s.' %(lang1, lang2, lang3)
```

```
message2 = 'The most popular programming languages
are %s, %s and %s.' %(lang1, lang3, lang2)

print(message1)
print(message2)
```

## Question 3

```
12
  12
```

In the second statement above, there are two spaces before the number 12.

## Question 4

```
1.725
  1.72
```

In the second statement above, there are three spaces before the number 1.72. This results in a total of 7 characters (three spaces, the digits 1, 7, 2 and the decimal point)

## Question 5

```
p, q = 111, 13
result = p/q

message = 'The result of %d divided by %d is %.3f,
correct to 3 decimal places.' %(p, q, result)

print(message)
```

In the solution above, we did not specify the total length of result when we use the %.3f formatter. This is acceptable as the specifying the total length is optional.

## Question 6

My name is Jamie and I am 31 years old.

## Question 7

My favorite colors are orange, blue and black.
My favorite colors are blue, orange and black.

## Question 8

```
student1 = 'Aaron'
student2 = 'Beck'
student3 = 'Carol'

message = 'My best friends are {}, {} and
{}.'.format(student1, student2, student3)

print(message)
```

## Question 9

 21.31 and 12
12 and 21.3124

In the first statement above, there are two spaces before the number 21.31.

## Question 10

```
x, y = 12, 7
quotient = x/y

message = 'The result of {} divided by {} is {:.4f},
correct to 4 decimal places.'.format(x, y, quotient)

print(message)
```

## Question 11

```
number = 2.7123
```

```
number = int(number)
print(number)
```

## Output

2

## Question 12

```
str(2.12431)
```

## Question 13

```
userInput = '12'
userInput = int(userInput)
print(userInput)
```

## Output

12

## Question 14

2
5

myList has 6 elements. Hence, only indexes from 0 to 5 are valid.

## Question 15

```
testScores = [10, 11, 12, 13]
print(testScores[3])
print(testScores[-1])
```

## Output

13
13

## Question 16

[1, 2, 3, 4, 5, 6, 7, 8, 9, 10]
[1, 2, 3, 4, 5, 6, 7, 8, 9, 10]
[4, 5, 6]
[1, 2, 3, 4, 5]
[3, 4, 5, 6, 7, 8, 9, 10]
[2, 4, 6]
[1, 4, 7, 10]

## Question 17

```
q17 = [11, 12, 13, 14, 15, 16, 17, 18, 19, 20]

sliceA = q17[2:8]
sliceB = q17[2: :3]

print(sliceA)
print(sliceB)
```

Output

[13, 14, 15, 16, 17, 18]
[13, 16, 19]

## Question 18

```
emptyList = []

emptyList.append(12)
emptyList.append(5)
emptyList.append(9)
emptyList.append(11)

print(emptyList)
```

Output

[12, 5, 9, 11]

## Question 19

```
q19 = [1, 2, 3, 4, 5]
q19[2] = 10
print(q19)
```

Output

[1, 2, 10, 4, 5]

## Question 20

```
q20 = ['A', 'B', 'C', 'D', 'E']

del q20[2]
del q20[0]

print(q20)
```

Output

['B', 'D', 'E']

It is easier to remove `'C'` first because if we remove `'A'` first, the indexes of the elements **after** `'A'` will change.

After removing `'A'`, q20 becomes `['B', 'C', 'D', 'E']`.

The index of `'C'` changes from 2 to 1.

In contrast, if we remove `'C'` first, only the indexes of elements after it (i.e. `'D'` and `'E'`) will be affected. The index of `'A'` remains unchanged.

## Question 21

```
daysOfWeek = ('Sun', 'Mon', 'Tues', 'Wed', 'Thurs', 'Fri', 'Sat')

myDay = daysOfWeek[2]
```

```
print(myDay)
```

Output

Tues

## Question 22

"John" is used as the dictionary key twice.

## Question 23

11
Zero
Three
{'Aaron': 12, 'Betty': 5, 0: 'Zero', 3.9: 'Three'}
{'Aaron': 12, 0: 'Zero', 3.9: 'Three'}

## Question 24

a) `dict1 = dict(One = 1, Two = 2, Three = 3, Four = 4, Five = 5)`
b) `print(dict1['Four'])`
c) `dict1['Three'] = 3.1`
d) `del dict1['Two']`
e) `print(dict1)`

Output

b) 4
e) {'One': 1, 'Three': 3.1, 'Four': 4, 'Five': 5}

## Question 25

```
capitals = {'USA':'Washington, D.C.', 'United
Kingdom':'London', 'China':'Beijing',
'Japan':'Tokyo', 'France':'Paris'}
print(capitals)
```

```
del capitals['China']
print(capitals)

capitals['Germany'] = 'Berlin'
capitals['Malaysia'] = 'Kuala Lumpur'
print(capitals)
```

Output

{'USA': 'Washington, D.C.', 'United Kingdom': 'London', 'China': 'Beijing', 'Japan': 'Tokyo', 'France': 'Paris'}

{'USA': 'Washington, D.C.', 'United Kingdom': 'London', 'Japan': 'Tokyo', 'France': 'Paris'}

{'USA': 'Washington, D.C.', 'United Kingdom': 'London', 'Japan': 'Tokyo', 'France': 'Paris', 'Germany': 'Berlin', 'Malaysia': 'Kuala Lumpur'}

# Chapter 5: Making Your Program Interactive

## Question 1

Determine the output of the following program without running the code:

```
a = 10
b = 4

print(a, "-", b, "=", a-b)
```

## Question 2

Rewrite the `print()` statement in Question 1 to display the same output using the % operator.

## Question 3

Rewrite the `print()` statement in Question 1 to display the same output using the `format()` method.

## Question 4

Determine the output of the following program without running the code:

```
print('''Date:\nJan 11, 2019

Time:\n1.28pm

Venue:\nConvention Center

Number of Pax:\n30''')
```

## Question 5

```
print('This is a single quotation (') mark and this
is a double quotation (") mark.')
```

The code above will result in a syntax error. Make the necessary amendment to correct it so that we get the following output:

*This is a single quotation (') mark and this is a double quotation (") mark.*

## Question 6

The code below shows the last few lines of a program:

```
print('Day 1 (%s): %s' %(day[1], venue[1]))
print('Day 2 (%s): %s' %(day[2], venue[2]))
print('Day 3 (%s): %s' %(day[3], venue[3]))
print('Day 4 (%s): %s' %(day[4], venue[4]))
print('Day 5 (%s): %s' %(day[5], venue[5]))
print('Day 6 (%s): %s' %(day[6], venue[6]))
print('Day 7 (%s): %s' %(day[7], venue[7]))
```

The lines before them are missing.

Add the missing lines so that the program prints the following output:

*Travel Itinerary*

*Day 1 (Tuesday): Tokyo to Osaka*
*Day 2 (Wednesday): Osaka*
*Day 3 (Thursday): Kyoto*
*Day 4 (Friday): Kyoto to Nara*
*Day 5(Saturday): Nara to Osaka*
*Day 6 (Sunday): Osaka to Tokyo*
*Day 7(Monday): Tokyo*

Hint: You need to use dictionaries in your solution.

## Question 7

Write a program that uses the `input()` function to prompt the user to enter an integer. Store the user's input into a variable called `num1`.

Next, prompt the user to enter another integer and store the input into another variable called `num2`.

Use the `print()` function to display the following message:

*You entered * and ^*

where * and ^ represent the two numbers entered by the user.

For instance, the program may behave as shown below (user input is in bold italics):

*Please enter an integer: 5*
*Please enter another integer: 12*

*You entered 5 and 12*

## Question 8

Use the `input()` function twice to prompt users to enter two integers and store the inputs into two variables called `in1` and `in2`.

Use the `int()` function to cast the inputs into integers and store the results back into `in1` and `in2`.

Calculate the average of the two numbers and assign the result to a variable called `average`. The average is found by adding the two numbers and dividing the result by 2.

Use the `print()` function to display the message

*The average is **

where * represents the value of `average`, correct to two decimal places.

For instance, the program may behave as shown below (user input is in bold italics):

*Please enter an integer:* **3**
*Please enter another integer:* **10**

*The average is 6.50*

## Question 9

Write a program that prompts the user to enter his/her name.

The program then prompts the user to enter his/her favorite number using the prompt below:

*Hi *, what is your favorite number?:*

where * is to be replaced by the user's name.

Finally, the program displays the message

*\*'s favorite number is ^.*

where * represents the user's name and ^ represents his/her favorite number.

For instance, the program may behave as shown below (user input is in bold italics):

*What is your name?:* **Jamie**
*Hi Jamie, what is your favorite number?:* **111**

*Jamie's favorite number is 111.*

# Question 10

Write a program that uses a dictionary to store the following information about a city and the country that it's in.

<u>City, Country</u>

Chicago, USA
Los Angeles, USA
New York, USA
Osaka, Japan
Tokyo, Japan
Shanghai, China
Moscow, Russia
Paris, France
London, England
Seoul, South Korea

The program then prompts the user to enter a city name from one of the 10 cities above. Based on the user's input, the program displays a message telling the user which country the city is located in.

For instance, the program may behave as shown below (user input is in bold italics):

*Cities: Chicago, Los Angeles, New York, Osaka, Tokyo, Shanghai, Moscow, Paris, London, Seoul*

*Please enter a city name from the list above:* ***Osaka***
*Osaka is located in Japan.*

# Question 11

Write a program that prompts the user to enter 5 numbers, separating the numbers with commas. Calculate the sum of the 5 numbers and display the numbers entered and the sum to the user.

For instance, the program may behave as shown below (user input is in bold italics):

*Please enter 5 numbers, separated by commas:* ***23, 1, 12, 4, 5***

*You entered 23, 1, 12, 4, 5.*
*The sum is 45.*

Hint: You can use the built-in Python method `split()` to work with the string input.

For instance, the statement

```
'1+24+51'.split('+')
```

uses a plus sign (+) as the delimiter to split the string

```
'1+24+51'
```

into the list

```
['1', '24', '51'].
```

For our question, you need to use a comma as the delimiter.

---

## Chapter 5: Answers

### Question 1

10 - 4 = 6

### Question 2

```
print("%d - %d = %d" % (a, b, a-b))
```

### Question 3

```
print("{} - {} = {}".format(a, b, a-b))
```

## Question 4

Date:
Jan 11, 2019

Time:
1.28pm

Venue:
Convention Center

Number of Pax:
30

## Question 5

```
print('This is a single quotation (\') mark and this
is a double quotation (") mark.')
```

## Question 6

```
day = {1:'Tuesday', 2:'Wednesday', 3:'Thursday',
4:'Friday', 5:'Saturday', 6:'Sunday', 7:'Monday'}

venue = {1:'Tokyo to Osaka', 2:'Osaka', 3:'Kyoto',
4:'Kyoto to Nara', 5:'Nara to Osaka', 6:'Osaka to
Tokyo', 7:'Tokyo'}

print('\nTravel Itinerary\n')
print('Day 1 (%s): %s' %(day[1], venue[1]))
print('Day 2 (%s): %s' %(day[2], venue[2]))
print('Day 3 (%s): %s' %(day[3], venue[3]))
print('Day 4 (%s): %s' %(day[4], venue[4]))
print('Day 5 (%s): %s' %(day[5], venue[5]))
print('Day 6 (%s): %s' %(day[6], venue[6]))
print('Day 7 (%s): %s' %(day[7], venue[7]))
```

## Question 7

```
num1 = input('Please enter an integer: ')
```

```
num2 = input('Please enter another integer: ')
print('You entered %s and %s' %(num1, num2))
```

## Question 8

```
in1 = input('Please enter an integer: ')
in2 = input('Please enter another integer: ')

in1 = int(in1)
in2 = int(in2)

average = (in1+in2)/2

print('The average is %.2f' %(average))
```

## Question 9

```
name = input('What is your name?: ')
favNum = input('Hi %s, what is your favorite number?:
' %(name))

print('%s\'s favorite number is %s.' %(name, favNum))
```

## Question 10

```
cities = {'Chicago':'USA', 'Los Angeles':'USA', 'New
York':'USA', 'Osaka':'Japan', 'Tokyo':'Japan',
'Shanghai':'China', 'Moscow':'Russia',
'Paris':'France', 'London':'England', 'Seoul':'South
Korea'}

print('Cities: Chicago, Los Angeles, New York, Osaka,
Tokyo, Shanghai, Moscow, Paris, London, Seoul')

print()

city = input('Please enter a city name from the list
above: ')

print('%s is located in %s.' %(city, cities[city]))
```

## Question 11

```
userInput = input('Please enter 5 numbers, separated
```

```
by commas: ')

inputList = userInput.split(',')

print('\nYou entered %s,%s,%s,%s,%s.' %(inputList[0],
inputList[1], inputList[2], inputList[3],
inputList[4]))

print('The sum is %d.' %(int(inputList[0]) +
int(inputList[1]) + int(inputList[2]) +
int(inputList[3]) + int(inputList[4])))
```

# Chapter 6: Making Choices and Decisions

## Question 1

State which of the following statements are true:

(a) `2 > 5`
(b) `9 < 11`
(c) `7 >= 3`
(d) `8 <= 8`
(e) `10 != 12`
(f) `6 == 3`
(g) `4 > 2 and 7!=9`
(h) `3 > 1 and 9==9 and 1 > 2`
(i) `2 > 3 or 5 > 1`
(j) `3 > 1 or 5 == 5`
(k) `3 > 1 or 10 != 8 or 9 < 2`

## Question 2

Determine the output of the following program without running the code:

```
num = 5

if num == 1:
    print('num is 1')
elif num == 2:
    print('num is 2')
else:
    print('num is neither 1 nor 2')
```

## Question 3

Use the `input()` function to prompt users to enter an integer and use the `int()` function to cast the input into an integer. Store the integer into a variable called `userInput`.

Next, write an `if` statement to perform the following tasks:

If `userInput` is positive, use the `print()` function to display the number entered.

If `userInput` is negative, multiply the number by -1 and assign it back to `userInput`. Next, use the `print()` function to display the new value of `userInput`.

Finally, if `userInput` is zero, use the `print()` function to display the message "You entered zero".

For instance, the program may behave as shown below (user input is in bold italics):

Example 1:
*Please enter an integer: 5*
*5*

Example 2:
*Please enter an integer: -2*
*2*

Example 3:
*Please enter an integer: 0*
*You entered zero*

## Question 4

Use the `input()` function to prompt users to enter an integer from 0 to 100 inclusive, cast the input into an integer and store the integer into a variable called `testScore`.

Use an `if` statement to display the grade that corresponds to `testScore` based on the following table:

70 to 100: A
60 to 69: B
50 to 59: C

0 to 49: Fail
Smaller than 0 or greater than 100: Invalid

For instance, the program may behave as shown below (user input is in bold italics):

Example 1:
*Please enter an integer from 0 to 100 inclusive:* ***20***
*Fail*

Example 2:
*Please enter an integer from 0 to 100 inclusive:* ***54***
*C*

Example 3:
*Please enter an integer from 0 to 100 inclusive:* ***-5***
*Invalid*

## Question 5

Determine the output of the following program without running the code:

```
num = 5

print('Orange Juice' if num == 5 else 'Peanut
Butter')
```

## Question 6

Use the `input()` function to prompt users to enter an integer, cast the input into an integer and store the integer into a variable called `num1`.

Write an inline `if` statement to print the message "Odd" or "Even" depending on whether `num1` is odd or even.

Hint: `num1` is even if the remainder is zero when it is divided by 2.

For instance, the program may behave as shown below (user input is in bold italics):

Example 1:
*Please enter an integer: **9***
*Odd*

Example 2:
*Please enter an integer: **18***
*Even*

## Question 7

Given that `myNumbers = [1, 21, 12, 45, 2, 7]`, use a `for` loop to print the elements in the list one by one.

## Question 8

Given that `marks = [12, 4, 3, 17, 20, 19, 16]`, use a `for` loop to find the sum of the numbers in the list. Use the `print()` function to print the sum.

## Question 9

Given that `classRanking = ['Jane', 'Peter', 'Michael', 'Tom']`, use a `for` loop and the `enumerate()` method to display the following output:

*1      Jane*
*2      Peter*
*3      Michael*
*4      Tom*

Each line consists of a number, <u>followed by a tab</u> and a name.

## Question 10

Given that `testScores = {'Aaron':12, 'Betty':17,`

`'Carol':14}`, write a `for` loop that gives us the following output:

*Aaron scored 12 marks.*
*Betty scored 17 marks.*
*Carol scored 14 marks.*

## Question 11

Determine the output of the following code without running the code:

```
ages = {'Abigail':7, 'Bond':13, 'Calvin':4}

for i, j in ages.items():
    print('%s\t%s' %(j, i))
```

## Question 12

Determine the output of the following code without running the code:

```
message = 'Happy Birthday'

for i in message:
    if (i == 'a'):
        print('@')
    else:
        print(i)
```

## Question 13

Determine the output of the following code without running the code:

(i)
```
for i in range(10):
    print (i)
```

(ii)
```
for i in range(2, 5):
    print(i)
```

(iii)
```
for i in range(4, 10, 2):
    print(i)
```

## Question 14

Explain what is wrong with the following code:

```
i = 0

while i < 5:
    print('The value of i = ', i)
```

Modify the code so that it produces the following output:

*The value of i = 0*
*The value of i = 1*
*The value of i = 2*
*The value of i = 3*
*The value of i = 4*

## Question 15

Determine the output of the following code without running the code:

```
i = 5

while i>0:
    if i%3 == 0:
        print(i, 'is a multiple of 3')
    else:
        print(i, 'is not a multiple of 3')

    i = i - 1
```

## Question 16

Write a while loop that repeatedly prompts users to enter a number or enter "END" to exit.

After the user enters the number, the while loop simply displays the number entered. If the user enters "END", the program displays the message "Goodbye!" and ends.

For instance, the program may behave as shown below (user input is in bold italics):

*Enter a number or END to exit:* ***3***
*3*

*Enter a number or END to exit:* ***123***
*123*

*Enter a number or END to exit:* ***-2***
*-2*

*Enter a number or END to exit:* ***END***
*Goodbye!*

## Question 17

Write a `while` loop that repeatedly prompts users to enter a positive integer or enter -1 to exit.

After the user enters the integer, the `while` loop should display the sum of all numbers entered so far. If the user enters -1, the program displays the message "Goodbye!" and ends.

For instance, the program may behave as shown below (user input is in bold italics):

*Enter a positive integer or -1 to exit:* ***3***
*Sum = 3*

*Enter a positive integer or -1 to exit:* ***5***
*Sum = 8*

*Enter a positive integer or -1 to exit:* ***1***
*Sum = 9*

*Enter a positive integer or -1 to exit: **-1***
*Goodbye!*

## Question 18

Modify the code in Question 17 so that if the user enters a non positive integer (other than -1), the program displays the message "You entered a non positive integer" and does not add the number to the sum.

For instance, the program may behave as shown below (user input is in bold italics):

*Enter a positive integer or -1 to exit: **3***
*Sum = 3*

*Enter a positive integer or -1 to exit: **5***
*Sum = 8*

*Enter a positive integer or -1 to exit: **-2***
*You entered a non positive integer*

*Enter a positive integer or -1 to exit: **4***
*Sum = 12*

*Enter a positive integer or -1 to exit: **-1***
*Goodbye!*

## Question 19

Write a program that prompts the user to enter two integers.

Suppose the integers are p and q. The program then prints p rows of q asterisks.

For instance, the program may behave as shown below (user input is in bold italics):

```
**********
**********
**********
**********
**********
```

Note: By default, the `print()` function adds a new line at the end of its output. If you do not want that to happen, you have to pass in `end = ''` to the `print()` function. This will remove the new line. Note that `''` is made up of two single quotes, not a single double quote.

For instance,

```
print('A')
print('B')
```

gives us

A
B

while

```
print('A', end = '')
print('B', end = '')
```

gives us

AB

**Question 20**

Write a program that prompts the user to enter a short message.

The program then replaces the first three occurrences of the letter "a" in the message with "@" and subsequent occurrences of the letter "a" with "A". Finally, the program displays the new message.

For instance, the program may behave as shown below (user input is in bold italics):

*Please enter a message:* ***Python is an excellent language to learn for both beginners and experienced programmers***

*Python is @n excellent l@ngu@ge to leArn for both beginners And experienced progrAmmers*

## Question 21

Write a program that uses a `for` loop to prompt the user to enter 10 numbers. The program then finds the smallest and largest number and displays the result to the user.

For instance, the program may behave as shown below (user input is in bold italics):

*Please enter number 1:* ***5***
*Please enter number 2:* ***12***
*Please enter number 3:* ***2***
*Please enter number 4:* ***3***
*Please enter number 5:* ***-1***
*Please enter number 6:* ***5.7***
*Please enter number 7:* ***11***
*Please enter number 8:* ***111***
*Please enter number 9:* ***0***
*Please enter number 10:* ***-3.9***

*The smallest number is -3.9*
*The largest number is 111*

## Question 22

Write a program that prompts the user to enter two integers, a and b. The program then calculates the product of all integers between a and b inclusive and displays the result to the user.

For instance, the program may behave as shown below (user input is in bold italics):

Example 1:
*Please enter the first integer:* **10**
*Please enter the second integer:* **13**

*17160*

Note:
10*11*12*13 = 17160

Example 2:
*Please enter the first integer:* **11**
*Please enter the second integer:* **6**

*332640*

## Question 23

Modify the program in Question 22 to satisfy the two rules below:

<u>Rule 1</u>

If 0 falls within a and b, it is <u>not multiplied</u> with the other numbers.

For instance, if a = -3 and b = 2, the program performs the calculation (-3)x(-2)x(-1)x1x2 without multiplying 0 with the other integers.

Rule 2

If the product is smaller than -500 or greater than 500, the program stops calculating and displays the message "Range Exceeded".

For instance, the program may behave as shown below (user input is in bold italics):

Example 1:
*Please enter the first integer: **-3***
*Please enter the second integer: **2***

*-12*

Example 2:
*Please enter the first integer: **11***
*Please enter the second integer: **6***

*Range Exceeded*

## Question 24

The code below leads to an infinite loop. Try modifying the code using the break keyword to exit the loop when users enter -1.

```
while 0==0:
    userInput = input('Press any key to continue or -
1 to exit: ')
    print('You entered', userInput)
```

## Question 25

Modify the code below using the continue keyword so that even numbers are not printed:

```
for i in range(10):
    print('i = ', i)
```

Hint: A number is even if the remainder is zero when it is divided by 2.

## Question 26

The factorial of a number n (denoted as n!) is given by the formula

$$n! = n(n-1)(n-2)(n-3)...(3)(2)(1)$$

For instance, $5! = 5x4x3x2x1 = 120$

Write a program that calculates the factorial of a number entered by the user.

The program should first prompt the user to enter a positive integer.

Next, the program checks if the input is positive. If it is, it calculates the factorial of that number and displays the result on the screen. Else, it displays the message "The number you entered is not positive".

For instance, the program may behave as shown below (user input is in bold italics):

Example 1:
*Enter a positive integer: 4*
24

Example 2:
*Enter a positive integer: -2*
*The number you entered is not positive*

## Question 27

With reference to Question 26 above, modify the program using a try-except statement so that if the user did not enter an integer, the program displays the message "You did not enter an integer".

For any other errors, the program displays the error messages pre-defined in Python.

For instance, the program may behave as shown below (user input is in bold italics):

*Enter a positive integer:* ***abcd***
*You did not enter an integer*

## Question 28

Given that `proLang = ['Python', 'Java', 'C', 'C++', 'C#', 'PHP', 'Javascript']`, write a program that uses a `try-except` statement to prompt the user to enter an integer.

The program displays "Out Of Range" if the user enters an integer that is beyond the index of the list.

For any other errors, the program displays the error messages that are pre-defined in Python.

If no error occurs, the program displays the item from the `proLang` list based on the index.

For instance, the program may behave as shown below (user input is in bold italics):

Example 1:
*Please enter the index:* ***3***
*C++*

Example 2:
*Please enter the index:* ***10***
*Out of Range*

Example 3:
*Please enter the index: **asdfa***
*invalid literal for int() with base 10: 'asdfa'.*

## Question 29

With reference to Question 10 in Chapter 5, modify the code so that the program repeatedly prompts the user to enter a city name or enter "END" to exit.

Based on the user's input, the program displays a message telling the user where the city is located in.

If the user enters a name that is not from the 10 cities listed, the program notifies the user that no result is found.

For instance, the program may behave as shown below (user input is in bold italics):

*Cities: Chicago, Los Angeles, New York, Osaka, Tokyo, Shanghai, Moscow, Paris, London, Seoul*

*Please enter a city name from the list above or enter END to exit:*
***Shanghai***
*Shanghai is located in China.*

*Please enter a city name from the list above or enter END to exit:*
***Berlin***
*Sorry, no result found.*

*Please enter a city name from the list above or enter END to exit:*
***END***

Hint: You can use a `try-except` statement to handle the error when the user enters a city that is not found.

## Chapter 6: Answers

## Question 1

(b), (c), (d), (e), (g), (i), (j) and (k) are true

## Question 2

num is neither 1 nor 2

## Question 3

```
userInput = int(input('Please enter an integer: '))

if userInput > 0:
    print(userInput)
elif userInput < 0:
    userInput = -1*userInput
    print(userInput)
else:
    print('You entered zero')
```

Note: In the first line of the code above, we use `input('Please enter an integer: ')` to prompt the user for an integer. This gives us the input as a string.

We pass this string to the `int()` function to cast it into an integer.

Here, we do the prompting and casting in one step. We can also break it down into two steps as shown below:

```
userInput = input('Please enter an integer: ')
userInput = int(userInput)
```

## Question 4

```
testScore = int(input('Please enter an integer from 0
to 100 inclusive: '))
```

```
if testScore > 100:
    print('Invalid')
elif testScore >= 70:
    print('A')
elif testScore >= 60:
    print('B')
elif testScore >= 50:
    print('C')
elif testScore >= 0:
    print('Fail')
else:
    print('Invalid')
```

## Question 5

Orange Juice

## Question 6

```
num1 = int(input('Please enter an integer: '))

print('Even' if num1%2 == 0 else 'Odd')
```

## Question 7

```
myNumbers = [1, 21, 12, 45, 2, 7]

for i in myNumbers:
    print (i)
```

<u>Output</u>

```
1
21
12
45
2
7
```

## Question 8

```
marks = [12, 4, 3, 17, 20, 19, 16]
```

```
sum = 0

for i in marks:
    sum = sum + i

print(sum)
```

## Output

91

## Question 9

```
classRanking = ['Jane', 'Peter', 'Michael', 'Tom']

for index, rank in enumerate(classRanking):
    print('%d\t%s' %(index+1, rank))
```

## Question 10

```
testScores = {'Aaron':12, 'Betty':17, 'Carol':14}

for i in testScores:
    print(i, 'scored', testScores[i], 'marks.')
```

## Question 11

```
7       Abigail
13      Bond
4       Calvin
```

## Question 12

```
H
@
p
p
y

B
i
```

r
t
h
d
@
y

## Question 13

(i)  0           (ii)  2
      1                3
      2                4
      3
      4           (iii)  4
      5                6
      6                8
      7
      8
      9

## Question 14

The `while` loop is an infinite loop because $i$ will always be smaller than 5.

The correct code should be:

```
i = 0

while i < 5:
    print('The value of i = ', i)
    i = i + 1
```

## Question 15

5 is not a multiple of 3
4 is not a multiple of 3
3 is a multiple of 3
2 is not a multiple of 3

1 is not a multiple of 3

## Question 16

```
userInput = input('Enter a number or END to exit: ')

while userInput != 'END':
    print(userInput)
    userInput = input('Enter a number or END to exit:
')

print('Goodbye!')
```

## Question 17

```
sum = 0
userInput = int(input('Enter a positive integer or -1
to exit: '))

while userInput != -1:
    sum += userInput
    print('Sum = ', sum)
    print()
    userInput = int(input('Enter a positive integer
or -1 to exit: '))

print('Goodbye!')
```

## Question 18

```
sum = 0
userInput = int(input('Enter a positive integer or -1
to exit: '))

while userInput != -1:
    if userInput <= 0:
        print('You entered a non positive integer.')
    else:
        sum += userInput
        print('Sum = ', sum)

    print()
    userInput = int(input('Enter a positive integer
or -1 to exit: '))
```

```
print('Goodbye!')
```

## Question 19

```
p = int(input('Please enter the number of rows: '))
q = int(input('Please enter the number of asterisks
per row: '))

for i in range(p):
    for j in range(q):
        print('*', end = '')
    print()
```

Let's look at an example of how this code works.

Suppose `p = 3` and `q = 5`.

The <u>outer</u> `for` loop

```
for i in range(p)
```

becomes

```
for i in range(3)
```

and loops from `i = 0` to `i = 2`.

The <u>inner</u> `for` loop

```
for j in range(q)
```

becomes

```
for j in range(5)
```

and loops from `j = 0` to `j = 4`.

This inner `for` loop is responsible for printing the asterisks. In our example, it loops from `j = 0` to `j = 4` and prints 5 asterisks

(**\*\*\*\*\***) using the line `print('*', end = '')`.

Once that is done, the inner `for` loop ends and the line `print()` is executed to move the cursor to the next line.

The outer `for` loop then increases the value of `i` by `1` and uses the inner `for` loop to print 5 asterisks again.

This is repeated from `i = 0` to `i = 2`.

Once that is done, a total of 3 lines of 5 asterisks will be printed on the screen.

## Question 20

```
message = input('Please enter a message: ')

j = 0

for i in message:
    if i == 'a':
        j = j + 1
        if j <= 3:
            print('@', end = '')
        else:
            print('A', end = '')
    else:
        print(i, end = '')

print()
```

Note: In the solution above, we use `j` to keep track of the number of occurrences of "a". Each time "a" occurs, we increment `j` by 1.

## Question 21

```
for i in range(10):
    userInput = input('Please enter number %d:
' % (i+1))
```

```
    #Assign the first user input
    #to largest and smallest
    if i == 0:
        largest = userInput
        smallest = userInput
    #From the second user input onwards,
    #compare user input with
    #current largest and smallest
    elif float(userInput) > float(largest):
        largest = userInput
    elif float(userInput) < float(smallest):
        smallest = userInput

print('The smallest number is %s' %(smallest))
print('The largest number is %s' %(largest))
```

Note: In the solution above, userInput, largest and smallest are all strings. Hence, we need to cast them into floats first before we can do any comparison.

## Question 22

```
a = int(input('Please enter the first integer: '))
b = int(input('Please enter the second integer: '))

'''if b is smaller than a, we swap the two numbers'''
if b<a:
    temp = b
    b = a
    a = temp

product = 1

for i in range(a, b+1):
    product = product*i

print(product)
```

## Question 23

```
a = int(input('Please enter the first integer: '))
b = int(input('Please enter the second integer: '))

'''if b is smaller than a, we swap the two numbers'''
if b<a:
```

```
    temp = b
    b = a
    a = temp

product = 1

for i in range(a, b+1):
    if i != 0:
        product = product*i
    if product > 500 or product < -500:
        product = -1
        break

if product == -1:
    print('Range Exceeded')
else:
    print(product)
```

## Question 24

```
while 0==0:
    userInput = input('Press any key to continue or -
1 to exit: ')
    if userInput == '-1':
        break
    else:
        print('You entered', userInput)
```

## Question 25

```
for i in range(10):
    if i%2 == 0:
        continue
    print('i = ', i)
```

Output

i = 1
i = 3
i = 5
i = 7
i = 9

## Question 26

```python
number = int(input('Enter a positive integer: '))

if number <= 0:
    print('The number you entered is not positive')
else:
    factorial = 1
    while number>0:
        factorial = number*factorial
        number -= 1
    print(factorial)
```

## Question 27

```python
try:
    number = int(input('Enter a positive integer: '))
    if number <= 0:
        print('The number you entered is not
positive')
    else:
        factorial = 1
        while number>0:
            factorial = number*factorial
            number -= 1
        print(factorial)
except ValueError:
    print('You did not enter an integer')
except Exception as e:
    print(e)
```

## Question 28

```python
proLang = ['Python', 'Java', 'C', 'C++', 'C#', 'PHP',
'Javascript']

try:
    index = int(input('Please enter the index: '))
    print(proLang[index])
except IndexError:
    print('Out of Range')
except Exception as e:
    print(e)
```

## Question 29

```
cities = {'Chicago':'USA', 'Los Angeles':'USA', 'New
York':'USA', 'Osaka':'Japan', 'Tokyo':'Japan',
'Shanghai':'China', 'Moscow':'Russia',
'Paris':'France', 'London':'England', 'Seoul':'South
Korea'}

print('Cities: Chicago, Los Angeles, New York, Osaka,
Tokyo, Shanghai, Moscow, Paris, London, Seoul')

print()

city = input('Please enter a city name from the list
above or enter END to exit: ')

while city != 'END':

    try:
        print('%s is located in %s.\n' %(city,
cities[city]))
        city = input('Please enter a city name from
the list above or enter END to exit: ')

    except:
        print('Sorry, no result found.\n')
        city = input('Please enter a city name from
the list above or enter END to exit: ')
```

Note that in the solution above, we have the statement

```
city = input('Please enter a city name from the list
above or enter END to exit: ')
```

in **both** the `try` and `except` blocks.

An alternative way is to use a `finally` block. A `finally` block is used for statements that should be executed regardless of whether the `try` or `except` block is executed.

The alternative solution is presented below:

```
cities = {'Chicago':'USA', 'Los Angeles':'USA', 'New
```

```python
York':'USA', 'Osaka':'Japan', 'Tokyo':'Japan',
'Shanghai':'China', 'Moscow':'Russia',
'Paris':'France', 'London':'England', 'Seoul':'South
Korea'}

print('Cities: Chicago, Los Angeles, New York, Osaka,
Tokyo, Shanghai, Moscow, Paris, London, Seoul')

print()

city = input('Please enter a city name from the list
above or enter END to exit: ')

while city != 'END':

    try:
        print('%s is located in %s.\n' %(city,
cities[city]))

    except:
        print('Sorry, no result found.\n')

    finally:
        city = input('Please enter a city name from
the list above or enter END to exit: ')
```

# Chapter 7: Functions and Modules

**Question 1**

Write a function called `greetUser()` that simply displays the message "Hello World" to users.

After coding the function, write a statement to call the function.

**Question 2**

Write a function called `greetUserByName()` that prompts the user for his/her name and displays the message

*Hello ^*

where ^ represents the name entered by the user.

After coding the function, write a statement to call the function.

**Question 3**

Write a function called `displayMessage()` that has one parameter `greetings`. Within the function, use the `print()` function to display the value of `greetings`.

After coding the function, write a statement to call the function using `'Good Morning'` as the argument.

**Question 4**

Write a function called `calculateQuotient()` that has two parameters `a` and `b`. Within the function, write a `return` statement to return the value of `a/b`.

After coding the function, write a statement to call the function using `12` and `3` as the arguments. Assign the result to a variable called `result` and print the value of `result`.

## Question 5

Modify the function in the previous question to include error handling using a `try-except` statement. Return -1 when an error occurs. Call this new function `calculateQuotient2()`.

After coding the function, write a statement to call the function using

(i) `12` and `3` as the arguments,
(ii) `5` and `0` as the arguments,
(iii) `'abcd'` and `2` as the arguments.

For each of the cases above, assign the result to a variable called `result` and print the value of `result`.

## Question 6

Write a function called `absValue()` that accepts a numerical input (the input can include decimal values).

If the input is zero or positive, it simply returns the number.

If the input is negative, it multiplies the number by -1 and returns the result.

If the input is non numerical, it returns -1.

After coding the function, call the function with the following inputs and print the results:

```
12
5.7
0
-4
-5.2
'abcd'
```

# Question 7

Determine the output of the following code without running the code:

```
a = 1
def displayNumbers():
    a = 2
    print(a)

displayNumbers()
print(a)
```

# Question 8

Explain what is wrong with the following code:

```
def functionwithb():
    b = 1
print(b)
```

# Question 9

Determine the output of the following code without running the code:

```
def calProduct(a, b, c = 1, d = 2):
    product = a*b*c*d
    print (product)

calProduct(2, 3)
calProduct(2, 3, 4)
calProduct(2, 3, 4, 5)
```

# Question 10

The statements below show the function teamMembers() being called with different arguments:

Function Call

```
teamMembers('Joanne', 'Lee')
```

Output

*The team members are Joanne, Lee, James and Kelly.*

Function Call

```
teamMembers('Benny', 'Aaron')
```

Output

*The team members are Benny, Aaron, James and Kelly.*

Function Call

```
teamMembers('Peter', 'John', 'Ben')
```

Output

*The team members are Peter, John, Ben and Kelly.*

Function Call

```
teamMembers('Jamie', 'Adam', 'Calvin', 'Danny')
```

Output

*The team members are Jamie, Adam, Calvin and Danny.*

Code the `teamMembers()` function to get the outputs shown and run it to verify that your function performs correctly.

## Question 11

Determine the output of the following code without running the code:

```
def findSum(*a):
    sum = 0
    for i in a:
        sum = sum + i

    print(sum)

findSum(1, 2, 3)
findSum(1, 2, 3, 4)
```

## Question 12

The statements below show the function `printFavColor()` being called with different arguments:

Function Call

```
printFavColor('Yellow', 'Green')
```

Output

*Your favorite colors are:*
*Yellow*
*Green*

Function Call

```
printFavColor('Orange', 'Pink', 'Blue')
```

Output

*Your favorite colors are:*
*Orange*
*Pink*
*Blue*

Code the `printFavColor()` function to get the outputs shown and run it to verify that your function performs correctly.

## Question 13

The statements below show the function
`printNamesAndGrades()` being called with different arguments.

Function Call

```
printNamesAndGrades(Adam = 'C', Tim = 'A')
```

Output

*Name : Grade*
*Adam : C*
*Tim : A*

Function Call

```
printNamesAndGrades(Sam = 'A-', Lee = 'B', Joan =
'A+')
```

Output

*Name : Grade*
*Sam : A-*
*Lee : B*
*Joan : A+*

Code the `printNamesAndGrades()` function to get the outputs
shown and run it to verify that your function performs correctly.

## Question 14

Explain what is wrong with the following code:

```
def varlengthdemo(*b, a, **c):
    print(a)
    for i in b:
        print (i)
    for j, k in c.items():
```

```
    print (j, 'scored', k)
```

Modify the `varlengthdemo()` function so that the statement

```
varlengthdemo('Jeremy', 2, 3, 4, Apple = 'A', Betty =
'B')
```

produces the following output:

*Jeremy*
*2*
*3*
*4*
*Apple scored A*
*Betty scored B*

Run the function to verify that it performs correctly.

## Question 15

Write a function called `sumOfTwoNumbers()` that has two parameters, `target` and `*b`.

The function checks if there exists any two numbers in `b` that add up to `target`.

If two numbers are found, the function displays an equation showing the addition.

If no numbers are found, the function prints the message "No result found".

For instance, the statements below show the function being called with different arguments.

Function Call

```
sumOfTwoNumbers(12, 3, 1, 4, 5, 6, 13)
```

<u>Output</u>

*No result found*

The function prints "No result found" for this example as it is unable to find any two numbers from 3, 1, 4, 5, 6, 13 that add up to the target 12.

<u>Function Call</u>

```
sumOfTwoNumbers(5, 3, 1, 4, 2)
```

<u>Output</u>

*3 + 2 = 5*

For this example, even though there can be more than one way to get the target 5 (1 + 4 and 3 + 2), the function is only required to display one equation.

Try coding this function and run it to verify that it performs correctly.

Hint: You can access the numbers in b using the list notation. For instance, for the function call

```
sumOfTwoNumbers(5, 3, 1, 4, 2)

target = 5
b[0] = 3
b[1] = 1
b[2] = 4
b[3] = 2
```

## Question 16

The statements below show the function `capitalsOfCountries()` being called with different arguments.

## Function Call

```
capitalsOfCountries(Germany = 'Berlin')
```

## Output

*The capital of Germany is Berlin.*

## Function Call

```
capitalsOfCountries(USA = 'Washington D.C.', China = 'Beijing')
```

## Output

*The capitals of USA and China are Washington D.C. and Beijing respectively.*

## Function Call

```
capitalsOfCountries(Japan = 'Tokyo', Indonesia = 'Jakarta', France = 'Paris')
```

## Output

*The capitals of Japan, Indonesia and France are Tokyo, Jakarta and Paris respectively.*

Code the `capitalsOfCountries()` function to get the outputs shown and run it to verify that your function performs correctly.

Note that the outputs produced by this function differ depending on the number of countries passed in. For instance, if there's only one country, the singular form is used (e.g. capital, is).

Hint:
You can use the `len()` method to find the number of items passed in to the `capitalsOfCountries()` function.

In addition, recall that you can use the `enumerate()` method to determine the index of the item that you are accessing when you loop through a dictionary.

For instance, if the dictionary is

```
capitals = {'USA':'Washington, D.C.', 'United
Kingdom':'London', 'China':'Beijing',
'Japan':'Tokyo', 'France':'Paris'}
```

and we use

```
for i, j in enumerate(capitals):
```

to loop through the `capitals` dictionary, `i` gives us the index of the current item while `j` gives us the dictionary key of the item.

In other words, when `i = 0, j = 'USA'`.

## Question 17

Suppose you have a file called *myfunctions.py* with the following code:

```
def func1():
    print('This is a simple function')

def func2(message):
    print(message)
```

The statements below show three ways of using functions from *myfunctions.py* inside another *.py* file **stored in the same folder**. Write down the correct `import` statement for each of them:

(i)
```
myfunctions.func1()
myfunctions.func2('Hello')
```

(ii)
```
f.func1()
f.func2('Hello')
```

(iii)
```
func1()
func2('Hello')
```

## Question 18

Now suppose we want to use `func1()` and `func2()` from the previous question inside a *.py* file that is NOT in the same folder as *myfunctions.py* and that *myfunctions.py* is stored in the *C:\PythonFiles* folder.

What code must we add to this new *.py* file so that we can continue to use the two functions?

---

## Chapter 7: Answers

## Question 1

```
def greetUser():
    print('Hello World')

greetUser()
```

Output

Hello World

## Question 2

```
def greetUserByName():
    name = input('Please enter your name: ')
    print('Hello %s' %(name))

greetUserByName()
```

Example of Output (user input is in bold italics)

Please enter your name: ***Jamie***
Hello Jamie

## Question 3

```
def displayMessage(greetings):
    print(greetings)

displayMessage('Good Morning')
```

Output

Good Morning

## Question 4

```
def calculateQuotient(a, b):
    return a/b

result = calculateQuotient(12, 3)
print(result)
```

Output

4.0

## Question 5

```
def calculateQuotient2(a, b):
    try:
        return a/b
    except:
        return -1

result = calculateQuotient2(12, 3)
print(result)

result = calculateQuotient2(5, 0)
print(result)
```

```
result = calculateQuotient2('abcd', 2)
print(result)
```

## Output

4.0
-1
-1

## Question 6

```
def absValue(a):
    try:
        num = float(a)
        if num >= 0:
            return a
        else:
            return -1*a
    except Exception as e:
        return -1

result = absValue(12)
print(result)

result = absValue(5.7)
print(result)

result = absValue(0)
print(result)

result = absValue(-4)
print(result)

result = absValue(-5.2)
print(result)

result = absValue('abcd')
print(result)
```

## Output

12
5.7

0
4
5.2
-1

## Question 7

2
1

## Question 8

b is defined inside `functionwithb()`.

Hence, it is not accessible outside the function when we try to print its value using `print(b)`.

## Question 9

12
48
120

## Question 10

```
def teamMembers(a, b, c = 'James', d = 'Kelly'):
    print('The team members are %s, %s, %s
and %s.' %(a, b, c, d))

teamMembers('Joanne', 'Lee')
teamMembers('Benny', 'Aaron')
teamMembers('Peter', 'John', 'Ben')
teamMembers('Jamie', 'Adam', 'Calvin', 'Danny')
```

## Question 11

6
10

## Question 12

```
def printFavColor(*color):
    print('Your favorite colors are:')
    for i in color:
        print(i)

printFavColor('Yellow', 'Green')
printFavColor('Orange', 'Pink', 'Blue')
```

## Question 13

```
def printNamesAndGrades(**grades):
    print('Name : Grade')
    for i in grades:
        print('%s : %s' %(i, grades[i]))

printNamesAndGrades(Adam = 'C', Tim = 'A')
printNamesAndGrades(Sam = 'A-', Lee = 'B', Joan =
'A+')
```

## Question 14

The `varlengthdemo()` function has a formal argument (a), a non-keyworded variable length argument (*b) and a keyworded variable length argument (**c).

When declaring the function, the formal argument must come first, followed by the non-keyworded argument and the keyworded argument (in that order).

The correct code is:

```
def varlengthdemo(a, *b, **c):
    print(a)
    for i in b:
        print (i)
    for j, k in c.items():
        print (j, 'scored', k)

varlengthdemo('Jeremy', 2, 3, 4, Apple = 'A', Betty =
'B')
```

## Question 15

```
def sumOfTwoNumbers(target, *b):

    length = len(b)

    for p in range(length-1):
        for q in range(p+1, length):
            if b[p] + b[q] == target:
                print(b[p],'+',b[q],'=', target)
                return
    print ('No result found')

sumOfTwoNumbers(12, 3, 1, 4, 5, 6, 13)

sumOfTwoNumbers(5, 3, 1, 4, 2)
```

Let's look at an example of how this function works.

Suppose `target = 5` and `b = [3, 1, 4, 2]`

The first line in the function sets `length` to 4 as there are 4 numbers in `b`.

The next line `for p in range(length - 1)` becomes `for p in range(3)`.

This causes the `for` loop to run from `p = 0` to `p = 2`.

When `p = 0`, the next line `for q in range(p+1, length)` becomes `for q in range(1, 4)`, which runs from `q = 1` to `q = 3`.

This means that the next line

```
if b[p] + b[q] == target:
```

becomes the following three `if` statements:

```
if b[0] + b[1] == target
```

```
if b[0] + b[2] == target
if b[0] + b[3] == target
```

Essentially, this means that when p = 0, we take b[0] (which is the first number in b) and add it to the subsequent numbers in b one by one. If any of the additions equals target, we have found the equation we need and can exit the function.

On the other hand, if we cannot find the equation that we need, we repeat the loop with p = 1. That is, we take b[1] (the second number in b) and add it to the subsequent numbers in b one by one.

We keep doing this until we reach p = 2. After p = 2, if we are still unable to find an equation, we've come to the end of the function and simply print the message "No result found" to notify the caller that we are unable to find the equation needed.

## Question 16

```
def capitalsOfCountries(**capitals):
    if(len(capitals) == 1):
        print('The capital of ', end = '')
    else:
        print('The capitals of ', end = '')

    # Print the country names
    for i, j in enumerate(capitals):
        if i == 0:
            print(j, end = '')
        elif i == len(capitals)-1:
            print(' and %s' % (j), end = '')
        else:
            print(', %s' % (j), end = '')

    if(len(capitals) == 1):
        print(' is ', end = '')
    else:
        print(' are ', end = '')

    # Print the capitals
    for i, j in enumerate(capitals):
```

```
        if i == 0:
            print(capitals[j], end = '')
        elif i == len(capitals)-1:
            print(' and %s' %(capitals[j]), end = '')
        else:
            print(', %s' %(capitals[j]), end = '')

    if len(capitals) == 1:
        print('.')
    else:
        print(' respectively.')

capitalsOfCountries(Germany = 'Berlin')
capitalsOfCountries(USA = 'Washington D.C.', China =
'Beijing')
capitalsOfCountries(Japan = 'Tokyo', Indonesia =
'Jakarta', France = 'Paris')
```

Most of the code above should be self-explanatory except for the `enumerate()` method.

The `enumerate()` method lets us know the index of the item that we are accessing in an iterable. For instance, in the code

```
for i, j in enumerate(capitals):
    if i == 0:
        print(j, end = '')
    elif i == len(capitals)-1:
        print(' and %s' %(j), end = '')
    else:
        print(', %s' %(j), end = '')
```

we use the `enumerate()` method to determine which item we are accessing from the `capitals` dictionary.

If it is the first item (`i == 0`), we print the country name.

If it is not the first item but is the last item (`i == len(capitals)-1`), we print the word "and", followed by the country name.

If it is neither the first nor the last item, we print a comma followed by the country name.

For instance, if
```
capitals = {'USA':'Washington, D.C.', 'United
Kingdom':'London', 'China':'Beijing'}
```

this segment of the code prints the following output:

USA, United Kingdom and China

## Question 17

(i) `import myfunctions`
(ii) `import myfunctions as f`
(iii) `from myfunctions import func1, func2`

## Question 18

```
import sys

if 'C:\\PythonFiles' not in sys.path:
    sys.path.append('C:\\PythonFiles')
```

# Chapter 8: Working with Files

**Question 1**

Create a text file called *ch8q1.txt* with the following text:

Top Students:
Carol
Zoe
Andy
Caleb
Xavier
Aaron
Ben
Adam
Betty

Write a simple program to read and display the ***first four lines*** from *ch8q1.txt*. The output should not have any blank lines between each line.

For this question, you can assume that *ch8q1.txt* is in the same folder as your *.py* file.

**Question 2**

Suppose we have a text file called *ch8q2.txt* that contains an unknown number of lines. Each line contains an integer.

Write a simple program to read the integers from *ch8q2.txt* and sum ***all the positive numbers***. Display the result of the sum.

Next, create the *ch8q2.txt* file as follows:

12
32
15

9
16
-3
45
-10

Run your code to verify that it works as intended. For this question, you can assume that *ch8q2.txt* is in the same folder as your *.py* file.

## Question 3

What is the difference between the `'w'` and `'a'` mode when using the `open()` function to work with files?

## Question 4

Write a function called `getNumbers()` that repeatedly prompts the user to enter an integer or enter "Q" to quit.

Write the integers that the user entered into a text file called *ch8q4.txt*, overwriting any previous data. You need to ensure that the user did indeed enter an integer before writing the value into *ch8q4.txt*.

Next, write another function called `findSum()` that reads from *ch8q4.txt*, adds up all the integers and returns the result.

Finally, call `getNumbers()` and `findSum()` and print the result returned by `findSum()`.

For this question, you can assume that *ch8q4.txt* is in the same folder as your *.py* file.

For instance, the program may behave as shown below (user input is in bold italics):

*Enter an integer or type Q to exit:* **1.11**
*Input is not an integer and will be ignored*
*Enter an integer or type Q to exit:* **1**
*Enter an integer or type Q to exit:* **12**
*Enter an integer or type Q to exit:* **123**
*Enter an integer or type Q to exit:* **-1**
*Enter an integer or type Q to exit:* **asfa**
*Input is not an integer and will be ignored*
*Enter an integer or type Q to exit:* **-11**
*Enter an integer or type Q to exit:* **Q**
*124*

## Question 5

Create a text file called *stars.txt* with a single line of 100 asterisks.

Use a `for` loop to read from the file and print the following output:

```
*
**
***
****
*****
******
*******
********
*********
```

For this question, you can assume that *stars.txt* is in the same folder as your *.py* file.

## Question 6

Suppose you have a folder on your *C:\* drive called *images*. Inside the *images* folder, you have a file called *happy.jpg*.

Write a program to read from *C:\images\happy.jpg* and write its content to a new file called *newhappy.jpg*.

For this question, you can write *newhappy.jpg* to the same folder as your *.py* file.

However, your *.py* file and *happy.jpg* should not be in the same folder (i.e. your *.py* file should not be in the *C:\images* folder).

Next, write code to change the name of the new file from *newhappy.jpg* to *happy.jpg* and delete the original *happy.jpg* file from *C:\images*.

---

## Chapter 8: Answers

### Question 1

```
f = open('ch8q1.txt', 'r')

for i in range(4):
    line = f.readline()
    print(line, end = '')

f.close()
```

Output

Top Students:
Carol
Zoe
Andy

### Question 2

```
f = open('ch8q2.txt', 'r')
sum = 0

for line in f:
    if int(line) > 0:
```

```
        sum = sum + int(line)

print(sum)

f.close()
```

Output

129

## Question 3

The 'w' mode is for writing to an output file. If the specified file does not exist, it will be created. If the specified file exists, any existing data on the file will be erased.

The 'a' mode is for appending to an output file. If the specified file does not exist, it will be created. If the specified file exists, any data written to the file is appended to the file (i.e. added to the end of the file).

## Question 4

```
def getNumbers():

    f = open('ch8q4.txt', 'w')

    userInput = input('Enter an integer or type Q to exit: ')

    while userInput != 'Q':
        try:
            num = int(userInput)
            f.write(userInput + '\n')
        except:
            print('Input is not an integer and will be ignored')
        finally:
            userInput = input('Enter an integer or type Q to exit: ')

    f.close()
```

```
def findSum():

    f = open('ch8q4.txt', 'r')
    sum = 0
    for line in f:
        sum = sum + int(line)

    f.close()

    return sum

getNumbers()
print(findSum())
```

## Question 5

```
f = open('stars.txt', 'r')

for i in range(9):
    line = f.read(i+1)
    print(line)

f.close()
```

## Question 6

```
from os import rename, remove

oldfile = open('C:\\images\\happy.jpg', 'rb')
newfile = open('newhappy.jpg', 'wb')

msg = oldfile.read(10)

while len(msg):
    newfile.write(msg)
    msg = oldfile.read(10)

oldfile.close()
newfile.close()

rename('newhappy.jpg', 'happy.jpg')
remove('C:\\images\\happy.jpg')
```

# Chapter 9: Object Oriented Programming Part 1

## Question 1

```
class Car:

    def __init__(self, pMake, pModel, pColor,
pPrice):
        self.make = pMake
        self.model = pModel
        self.color = pColor
        self.price = pPrice

    def __str__(self):
        return 'Make = %s, Model = %s, Color = %s,
Price = %s' %(self.make, self.model, self.color,
self.price)

    def selectColor(self):
        self.color = input('What is the new color? ')

    def calculateTax(self):
        priceWithTax = 1.1*self.price
        return priceWithTax
```

Copy the code above into a file called *car.py*. Within the same file, but outside the `Car` class, write code for each of the following tasks:

(a) Instantiate a `Car` object called `myFirstCar` with the following values:

```
make = 'Honda'
model = 'Civic'
color = 'White'
price = 15000
```

(b) Print a string representation of `myFirstCar` using the `__str__` method. You should get

*Make = Honda, Model = Civic, Color = White, Price = 15000*

as the output.

(c) Update the price of `myFirstCar` to 18000 and print a string representation of it again.

(d) Update the color of `myFirstCar` to "Orange" using the `selectColor()` method and print a string representation of it again.

(e) Use `myFirstCar` to call the `calculateTax()` method and assign the result to a variable called `finalPrice`. Print the value of `finalPrice`.

**Question 2**

(a) Write a class called `Room` that has four instance variables, `size`, `view`, `type` and `basicRates`.

Within the class, you need to have the __init__ and __str__ methods.

(b) Next, write an instance method called `calculateRates()` within the `Room` class.

The `calculateRates()` method has a parameter (in addition to `self`) called `day`. Based on the value of `day`, the method multiplies `basicRates` by a certain factor.

If `day` equals `'Weekends'`, it multiplies `basicRates` by 1.5
If `day` equals `'Public Holidays'`, it multiplies it by 2.
If `day` equals `'Christmas'`, it multiplies it by 2.5.
For any other values of `day`, it multiplies it by 1.

After multiplying, the method returns the result.

(c) Next, outside the class, instantiate a `Room` object called `room1` with `size = 132`, `view = 'City'`, `type = 'Double'` and `basicRates = 120` and print a string representation of `room1`.

(d) Use `room1` to call the `calculateRates()` method, using `'Public Holidays'` as the argument. Assign the result to a variable called `newRates` and print the value of `newRates`.

## Question 3

(a) For the code below, add a property called `bonus` for the instance variable `_bonus`.

```
class HumanResource:
    def __init__(self, pName, pSalary, pBonus):
        self.name = pName
        self.salary = pSalary
        self._bonus = pBonus

    def __str__(self):
        return 'Name = %s, Salary = %.2f, Bonus
= %.2f' % (self.name, self.salary, self._bonus)
```

The getter method of the property simply returns the value of `_bonus`.

The setter method, on the other hand, allows us to set the value of `_bonus`. If we try to set it to a negative value, the setter method should display the message

*Bonus cannot be negative.*

(b) Outside the class, instantiate a `HumanResource` object called `chiefOps` with the following values:

```
name = 'Kelly'
salary = 715000
_bonus = 0
```

(c) Use the `bonus` **property** to set `_bonus` to -20 for `chiefOps`.

Verify that you get the message "Bonus cannot be negative".

(d) Next, use the `bonus` property to change _bonus to 50000. and use the getter method of the property to verify that _bonus is set correctly.

## Question 4

```
class NameManglingDemo:
    def __init__(self):
        self.__myData = 1
```

In the code above, `myData` is preceded by two leading underscores. What is the mangled name for `myData`?

## Question 5

(a) What is the difference between a class variable and an instance variable?

(b) With reference to the code below, list the instance and class variable(s).

```
class Book:
    message = 'Welcome to Books Online'

    def __init__(self, pTitle, pAuthor, pPrice):
        self.title = pTitle
        self.author = pAuthor
        self.price = pPrice

    def __str__(self):
        return 'Title = %s, Author = %s, Price
= %.2f' % (self.title, self.author, self.price)
```

(c) With reference to the `Book` class in part (b), determine the output of the following code without running the code:

```
aRomanceBook = Book('Sunset', 'Jerry', 10)
aSciFiBook = Book('Viz', 'Lee', 10)
```

```
aRomanceBook.price = 20
print(aRomanceBook.price)
print(aSciFiBook.price)

Book.message = 'Books Online'
print(aRomanceBook.message)
print(aSciFiBook.message)
```

## Question 6

(a) Write a class called `Student` that has two instance variables, `name` and `marks`, and one class variable, `passingMark`. Assign 50 to `passingMark`.

Within the class, you need to code the __init__ and __str__ methods.

(b) Next, write an instance method called `passOrFail()` within the `Student` class. This method returns the string "Pass" if `marks` is greater than or equal to `passingMark` or "Fail" if `marks` is lower than `passingMark`.

(c) Outside the class, instantiate a `Student` object called `student1` with `name` = `'John'` and `marks` = `52` and use it to call the `passOrFail()` method. Assign the result to a variable called `status1` and print the value of `status1`.

(d) Instantiate another `Student` object called `student2` with `name` = `'Jenny'` and `marks` = `69` and use it to call the `passOrFail()` method. Assign the result to a variable called `status2` and print the value of `status2`.

(e) Update the value of `passingMark` to `60` for all instances of the `Student` class and call the `passOrFail()` method for `student1` and `student2` again. Assign the results to `status1` and `status2` respectively and print the two values.

# Question 7

(a) What is the difference between an instance method, a class method and a static method?

(b) In the code below, which is an instance method and which is a class method?

```
class MethodsDemo:
    message = 'Class message'

    def __init__(self, pMessage):
        self.message = pMessage

    @classmethod
    def printMessage(cls):
        print(cls.message)

    def printAnotherMessage(self):
        print(self.message)
```

(c) Given that `md1 = MethodsDemo('md1 Instance Message')`, what are the two ways to call the class method?

(d) Add a static method called `printThirdMessage()` to the `MethodsDemo` class that simply prints the message "This is a static method".

(e) What are the two ways to call the static method in part d?

# Question 8

Create a class called `Movies` that stores information about movies. The class should store the following information: the title of the movie, its genre, the main language it is in, the director(s) and the year it was first released.

The class should also have the __init__ and __str__ methods.

In addition, the class should have a property that allows users to get and set the genre of the movie. The setter method should only allow users to set the genre to `'Romance'`, `'Action'`, `'Drama'`, `'Thriller'` or `'Horror'`. If the user tries to set the genre to anything else, the setter method should display an appropriate error message to the user.

Next, we need an instance method called `recommendMovie()` that recommends users a new movie to watch based on the genre of the instance used to call the method.

If the genre is `'Romance'`, the movie `'First Date'` is recommended.

If the genre is `'Action'`, the movie `'Mutant'` is recommended.

If the genre is `'Drama'`, the movie `'The Awakening'` is recommended.

If the genre is `'Thriller'`, the movie `'Mr K'` is recommended.

If the genre is `'Horror'`, the movie `'A walk down Dawson Street'` is recommended.

This method should display the recommended movie on the screen.

Save the code above into a file called *movie.py*.

Next, create another file called *main.py* and import the `Movies` class into this file.

Instantiate a `Movies` instance called `mov1` with the following information:

Title of the movie = `'And so it begins'`
Genre = `' '`
Main language = `'English'`

Director = 'Robert Kingman, Joe Patterson'
Year it was first released = 2019

After creating mov1, set its genre to 'Fantasy'. This should fail. Next, set the genre to 'Romance' and print a string representation of mov1.

Finally, use mov1 to call the recommendMovie() method.

---

## Chapter 9: Answers

### Question 1

(a)
```
myFirstCar = Car('Honda', 'Civic', 'White', 15000)
```

(b)
```
print(myFirstCar)
```

(c)
```
myFirstCar.price = 18000
print(myFirstCar)
```

Output

Make = Honda, Model = Civic, Color = White, Price = 18000

(d)
```
myFirstCar.selectColor()
print(myFirstCar)
```

Output

What is the new color? **Orange**
Make = Honda, Model = Civic, Color = Orange, Price = 18000

## (e)

```
finalPrice = myFirstCar.calculateTax()
print(finalPrice)
```

Output

19800.0

## Question 2

### (a) and (b)

```
class Room:

    def __init__(self, pSize, pView, pType,
pBasicRates):
        self.size = pSize
        self.view = pView
        self.type = pType
        self.basicRates = pBasicRates

    def __str__(self):
        return 'Size = %s sq ft\nView = %s\nType
= %s\nBasic Rates = USD%s' %(self.size, self.view,
self.type, self.basicRates)

    def calculateRates(self, day):
        if day == 'Weekends':
            return 1.5*self.basicRates
        elif day == 'Public Holidays':
            return 2*self.basicRates
        elif day == 'Christmas':
            return 2.5*self.basicRates
        else:
            return 1*self.basicRates
```

### (c)

```
room1 = Room(132, 'City', 'Double', 120)
print(room1)
```

Output

Size = 132 sq ft
View = City

Type = Double
Basic Rates = USD120

(d)
```
newRates = room1.calculateRates('Public Holidays')
print(newRates)
```

<u>Output</u>

240

## Question 3

(a)
```
class HumanResource:
    def __init__(self, pName, pSalary, pBonus):
        self.name = pName
        self.salary = pSalary
        self._bonus = pBonus

    def __str__(self):
        return 'Name = %s, Salary = %.2f, Bonus
= %.2f' %(self.name, self.salary, self._bonus)

    @property
    def bonus(self):
        return self._bonus

    @bonus.setter
    def bonus(self, value):
        if value < 0:
            print('Bonus cannot be negative')
        else:
            self._bonus = value
```

(b)
```
chiefOps = HumanResource('Kelly', 715000, 0)
```

(c)
```
chiefOps.bonus = -20
```

Output

Bonus cannot be negative

(d)
```
chiefOps.bonus = 50000
print(chiefOps.bonus)
```

Output

50000

## Question 4

```
_NameManglingDemo__myData
```

## Question 5

(a)
A class variable belongs to the class and is shared by all instances of that class. It is defined outside any method in the class. We can access it by prefixing the variable name with the class name.

An instance variable, on the other hand, is defined inside a method and belongs to an instance. It is always prefixed with the `self` keyword.

(b)
`title`, `author` and `price` are instance variables.
`message` is a class variable.

(c)
20
10
Books Online
Books Online

# Question 6

## (a) and (b)

```
class Student:

    passingMark = 50

    def __init__(self, pName, pMarks):
        self.name = pName
        self.marks = pMarks

    def __str__(self):
        return 'Name of Student = %s\nMarks
= %d' % (self.name, self.marks)

    def passOrFail(self):
        if self.marks >= Student.passingMark:
            return 'Pass'
        else:
            return 'Fail'
```

## (c)

```
student1 = Student('John', 52)
status1 = student1.passOrFail()
print(status1)
```

Output

Pass

## (d)

```
student2 = Student('Jenny', 69)
status2 = student2.passOrFail()
print(status2)
```

Output

Pass

## (e)

```
Student.passingMark = 60
status1 = student1.passOrFail()
print(status1)
```

```
status2 = student2.passOrFail()
print(status2)
```

Output

Fail
Pass

## Question 7

(a)
An instance method has an instance of the class as its first parameter. `self` is commonly used to represent this instance.

A class method, on the other hand, has a class object (instead of `self`) as its first parameter. `cls` is commonly used to represent that class object.

A static method is a method that is not passed an instance or a class object (i.e. it is not passed `self` or `cls`).

To call an instance method, we use the instance name.

To call a static or class method, we can use the class name or instance name.

(b)
`printAnotherMessage()` is an instance method
`printMessage()` is a class method.

(c)
`md1.printMessage()` or `MethodsDemo.printMessage()`

Output

Class message
Class message

(d)

```
class MethodsDemo:
    message = 'Class message'

    def __init__(self, pMessage):
        self.message = pMessage

    @classmethod
    def printMessage(cls):
        print(cls.message)

    def printAnotherMessage(self):
        print(self.message)

    @staticmethod
    def printThirdMessage():
        print('This is a static method')
```

(e)

```
md1.printThirdMessage() or
MethodsDemo.printThirdMessage()
```

Output

This is a static method
This is a static method

## Question 8

*movie.py*

```
class Movies:
    def __init__(self, pTitle, pGenre, pLanguage,
pDirectors, pYear):
        self.title = pTitle
        self._genre = pGenre
        self.language = pLanguage
        self.directors = pDirectors
        self.year = pYear

    def __str__(self):
        return 'Title = %s\nGenre = %s\nLanguage
= %s\nDirectors = %s\nYear = %s\n' %(self.title,
```

```
self._genre, self.language, self.directors,
self.year)

    @property
    def genre(self):
        return self._genre

    @genre.setter
    def genre(self, value):
        if value in ['Romance', 'Action', 'Drama',
'Thriller', 'Horror']:
            self._genre = value
        else:
            print ('%s is an invalid
genre.\n' %(value))

    def recommendMovie(self):
        recommendations = {'Romance':'First Date',
'Action':'Mutant', 'Drama':'The Awakening',
'Thriller':'Mr K', 'Horror':'A walk down Dawson
Street'}
        print ('You may also like the following
movie: %s.' %(recommendations[self._genre]))
```

### *main.py*

```
from movie import Movies

mov1 = Movies('And so it begins', '', 'English',
'Robert Kingman, Joe Patterson', 2019)

mov1.genre = 'Fantasy'

mov1.genre = 'Romance'
print(mov1)
mov1.recommendMovie()
```

## Output

Fantasy is an invalid genre.

Title = And so it begins
Genre = Romance
Language = English

Directors = Robert Kingman, Joe Patterson
Year = 2019

You may also like the following movie: First Date.

# Chapter 10: Object Oriented Programming Part 2

## Question 1

Create a file called *shape.py* and save it onto your desktop. Add the following code to the file:

```
class Shape:
    def __init__(self, pType, pArea):
        self.type = pType
        self.area = pArea
    def __str__(self):
        return '%s of area %4.2f units
square' %(self.type, self.area)

class Square(Shape):
    def __init__(self, pLength):
        super().__init__('Square', 0)
        self.length = pLength
        self.area = self.length*self.length
```

The code above consists of two classes – Shape and Square.

Square is a subclass that inherits from Shape. This subclass only has one method __init__, with two parameters self and pLength.

Within the method, we first call the __init__ method from the parent class (using the super() function), passing in 'Square' and 0 as arguments.

These arguments are used to initialized the instance variables type and area in the parent class, which the subclass class inherits.

Next, we assign the parameter pLength to a new instance variable called length. In addition, we calculate the area of a square and use it to update the value of the inherited instance variable area.

(Note: The area of a square is given by the square of its length).

Study the code above and make sure you fully understand it.

a) Next, we need to add two more subclasses, `Triangle` and `Circle`, to *shape.py*. Both subclasses have one method: `__init__`.

You need to decide on the appropriate parameter(s) for these methods.

Both `__init__` methods should call the `__init__` method in the parent class and pass in appropriate values for the inherited instance variables `type` and `area`.

In addition, they should have their own instance variables and contain a statement for updating the value of the inherited instance variable `area`.

Try modifying the `Square` subclass yourself to code the `Triangle` and `Circle` subclasses.

Hint:

A triangle is defined by its base and height and its area is given by the mathematical formula 0.5*base*height.

A circle is defined by its radius and its area is given by the mathematical formula π*radius*radius.

π is a constant represented as `math.pi` in the `math` module. You need to import the `math` module to get the value of π.

b) After coding the subclasses, create another file on your desktop and name it *shapemain.py*.

Within *shapemain.py*, import the classes in *shape.py* and

instantiate one instance of each subclass using the following information:

A `Square` instance called `sq` with a length of 5.

A `Circle` instance called `c` with a radius of 10.

A `Triangle` instance called `t` with a base of 12 and a height of 4.

c) Use the `print()` function to display information about each instance.

## Question 2

In this question, we shall modify the `Shape` class in Question 1 by adding one more method to it - the __add__ method.

This method has two parameters, `self` and `other`, and overrides the + operator. Instead of performing basic addition, the + operator should return the sum of the areas of two `Shape` instances. In other words, if one instance has an area of 11.1 and another has an area of 7.15, the __add__ method should return the value 18.25.

Add the __add__ method to the `Shape` class in *shape.py*.

Next, use the `print()` function in *shapemain.py* to verify that `sq` + `c` gives you the sum of the areas of `sq` and `c`.

## Question 3

In this question, we'll try to use the __add__ method in Question 2 to find the sum of the areas of `sq`, `c` and `t`.

Try doing `print(sq + c + t)` in *shapemain.py*. What happens? You get an error, right?

This is because the + operator is trying to do `sq + c` first, before adding the result to `t`.

However, notice that `sq + c` gives us a numerical value, which is the result of `sq.area + c.area`.

When we try to add `sq + c` to `t`, we get an error because the + operator is unable to add `sq + c` (which is a float) to `t` (which is a `Triangle` instance).

If you study the __add__ method, you'll see that the + operator expects both the arguments (for the `self` and `other` parameters) to be instances of the `Shape` class (or instances of subclasses of the `Shape` class).

To overcome this, we need to change the __add__ method. Instead of returning a numerical result, we need it to return a `Shape` instance so that we can pass this result to the + operator again to do further additions.

To do that, we'll change the

```
return self.area + other.area
```

statement in the __add__ method to

```
return Shape ('New Shape', self.area + other.area)
```

Next, in *shapemain.py*, try doing `print(sq + c + t)` again and verify that you get a new `Shape` instance (`type = 'New Shape'`) whose area is the sum of the areas of `sq`, `c` and `t`.

## Question 4

In this question, we need to create a class called `Student`.

This class has 4 instance variables: `name`, `id`, `course_enrolled` and `annual_fees`.

Within the class, we need to have an `__init__` method to initialize the 4 instance variables. We also need to have a `__str__` method.

Try coding this class yourself.

Next, we'll inherit three subclasses from `Student`.

The first subclass is `ArtsStudent`. It has an additional instance variable called `project_grade`.

The second subclass is `CommerceStudent`. It has an additional instance variable called `internship_company`.

The third subclass is `TechStudent`. It has two additional instance variables called `internship_company` and `project_grade`.

Try coding these three subclasses yourself. Each subclass should override the `__init__` and `__str__` methods in the parent class. They should also use the `super()` function to reuse code from the parent class.

Last but not least, we need to add the `__lt__` and `__gt__` methods to our parent class. These are special methods in Python that allow us to make comparisons.

`lt` stands for "less than" while `gt` stands for "greater than". They override the < and > operators respectively.

Add these two methods to the `Student` class so that they allow us to compare the annual fees (stored in the instance variable `annual_fees`) of two instances and return `True` or `False` accordingly. For instance, if we have the following code,

```
student1 = ArtsStudent('Jim', 'A19001', 'Psychology', 12000, 'In Progress')
```

```
student2 = CommerceStudent('Ben', 'C19011',
'Marketing', 15000, 'Cool Mart')
```

student1 > student2 should give us False as the
annual_fees of student1 is lower than that of student2.

In contrast, student1 < student2 should give us True.

Once that is done, save the file as *student.py* on your desktop.
Next, create another file called *ch10q4.py* on your desktop and
import the classes in *student.py*.

Instantiate three instances with the following information and
print a string representation of each instance:

ArtsStudent instance named as1

```
name = 'Peter Johnson'
id = 'A19012'
course_enrolled = 'History'
annual_fees = 11000
project_grade =  'A'
```

CommerceStudent instance named cs1

```
name = 'Alan Goh'
id = 'C19111'
course_enrolled = 'Digital Marketing'
annual_fees = 13400
internship_company = 'Digital Consultancy'
```

TechStudent instance named ts1

```
name = 'Larry Faith'
id = 'T19126'
course_enrolled = 'Computer Science'
annual_fees = 21000
project_grade = 'A'
internship_company = 'Kyla Tech'
```

Finally, use the > or < operator to compare the annual fees of ts1 vs `cs1`.

Use an `if-else` statement to display the message

*The annual fees of a technical student is higher than that of a commerce student.*

if the annual fees of `ts1` is greater than that of `cs1`.

Else, display the message

*The annual fees of a technical student is lower than that of a commerce student.*

---

## Chapter 10: Answers

### Question 1

(a)
*shape.py*

```python
import math

# Shape class

class Shape:
    def __init__(self, pType, pArea):
        self.type = pType
        self.area = pArea
    def __str__(self):
        return '%s of area %4.2f units
square' %(self.type, self.area)

# Square subclass

class Square(Shape):
    def __init__(self, pLength):
        super().__init__('Square', 0)
        self.length = pLength
        self.area = self.length*self.length
```

```
# Triangle subclass

class Triangle(Shape):
    def __init__(self, pBase, pHeight):
        super().__init__('Triangle', 0)
        self.base = pBase
        self.height = pHeight
        self.area = 0.5*self.base*self.height

# Circle subclass

class Circle(Shape):
    def __init__(self, pRadius):
        super().__init__('Circle', 0)
        self.radius = pRadius
        self.area = math.pi*self.radius*self.radius
```

(b)

*shapemain.py*

```
from shape import Square, Circle, Triangle

sq = Square(5)
c = Circle(10)
t = Triangle(12, 4)
```

(c)
```
print(sq)
print(c)
print(t)
```

Output

Square of area 25.00 units square
Circle of area 314.16 units square
Triangle of area 24.00 units square

**Question 2**

*shape.py* (added to the `Shape` class)

```
    def __add__(self, other):
```

```
      return self.area + other.area
```

*shapemain.py*

```
print(sq + c)
```

Output

339.1592653589793

## Question 3

*shape.py* (the modified __add__ method)

```
    def __add__(self, other):
        return Shape ('New Shape', self.area +
other.area)
```

*shapemain.py*

```
print(sq + c + t)
```

Output

New Shape of area 363.16 units square

## Question 4

*student.py*

```
# Student Class

class Student:

    def __init__(self, pName, pID, pCourseEnrolled,
pAnnualFees):
        self.name = pName
        self.id = pID
        self.course_enrolled = pCourseEnrolled
        self.annual_fees = pAnnualFees
```

```python
    def __str__(self):
        return 'Name = %s\nID = %s\nCourse Enrolled
= %s\nAnnual Fees = %s' %(self.name, self.id,
self.course_enrolled, self.annual_fees)

    def __lt__(self, other):
        return self.annual_fees < other.annual_fees

    def __gt__(self, other):
        return self.annual_fees > other.annual_fees

# ArtsStudent subclass

class ArtsStudent(Student):

    def __init__(self, pName, pID, pCourseEnrolled,
pAnnualFees, pProjectGrade):
        super().__init__(pName, pID, pCourseEnrolled,
pAnnualFees)
        self.project_grade = pProjectGrade

    def __str__(self):
        return super().__str__() + '\nProject Grade
= %s' %(self.project_grade)

# CommerceStudent subclass

class CommerceStudent(Student):

    def __init__(self, pName, pID, pCourseEnrolled,
pAnnualFees, pInternshipCompany):
        super().__init__(pName, pID, pCourseEnrolled,
pAnnualFees)
        self.internship_company = pInternshipCompany

    def __str__(self):
        return super().__str__() + '\nInternship
Company = %s' %(self.internship_company)

# TechStudent subclass

class TechStudent(Student):

    def __init__(self, pName, pID, pCourseEnrolled,
pAnnualFees, pProjectGrade, pInternshipCompany):
        super().__init__(pName, pID, pCourseEnrolled,
```

```
                pAnnualFees)
        self.project_grade = pProjectGrade
        self.internship_company = pInternshipCompany

    def __str__(self):
        return super().__str__() + '\nProject Grade
= %s\nInternship Company = %s' %(self.project_grade,
self.internship_company)
```

### *ch10q4.py*

```
import student

as1 = student.ArtsStudent('Peter Johnson', 'A19012',
'History', 11000, 'A')
cs1 = student.CommerceStudent('Alan Goh', 'C19111',
'Digital Marketing', 13400, 'Digital Consultancy')
ts1 = student.TechStudent('Larry Faith', 'T19126',
'Computer Science', 21000, 'A', 'Kyla Tech')

print(as1)
print()
print(cs1)
print()
print(ts1)
print()

if ts1 > cs1:
    print('The annual fees of a technical student is
higher than that of a commerce student.')
else:
    print('The annual fees of a technical student is
lower than that of a commerce student.')
```

### Output

Name = Peter Johnson
ID = A19012
Course Enrolled = History
Annual Fees = 11000
Project Grade = A

Name = Alan Goh
ID = C19111
Course Enrolled = Digital Marketing
Annual Fees = 13400
Internship Company = Digital Consultancy

Name = Larry Faith
ID = T19126
Course Enrolled = Computer Science
Annual Fees = 21000
Project Grade = A
Internship Company = Kyla Tech

The annual fees of a technical student is higher than that of a commerce student.

# Project 1

Now that you have completed the exercises for all the chapters, let's work on two projects.

## Spelling Out Numbers Part 1

The first project is easy to explain; we need to write a program that spells out any integer up to 3 digits (i..e any integer less than 1000). For instance, if the user keys in 729, the program should display

*Seven Hundred and Twenty Nine*

You can use any of the concepts you've learned in the previous chapters. Try coding it yourself. If you are stuck, you can refer to the suggested solution for help.

## Suggested Solution

```
# Defining the printText() function

def printText(userInput):

    unitsMapping = {'0':'', '1':' One', '2':' Two',
'3':' Three', '4':' Four', '5':' Five', '6':' Six',
'7':' Seven', '8':' Eight', '9':' Nine'}

    tensMapping = {'0':'', '2':' Twenty', '3':'
Thirty', '4':' Forty', '5':' Fifty', '6':' Sixty',
'7':' Seventy', '8':' Eighty', '9':' Ninety'}

    teensMapping = {'10':' Ten', '11':' Eleven',
'12':' Twelve', '13':' Thirteen', '14':' Fourteen',
'15':' Fifteen', '16':' Sixteen', '17':' Seventeen',
'18':' Eighteen', '19':' Nineteen'}

    # Getting the length of number
    numLength = len(userInput)
    numText = ''
```

```python
    # Getting the digits for each place value
    units = userInput[numLength - 1] if numLength >=
1 else '0'

    tens = userInput[numLength - 2] if numLength >= 2
else '0'

    hundreds = userInput[numLength - 3] if
numLength >= 3 else '0'

    '''
    This comment block is to be replaced
    with code in Part 2
    Leave it as it is now
    '''

    #Printing the hundreds
    if (hundreds != '0'):
        numText = numText + unitsMapping[hundreds] +
' Hundred'

    #Adding "and" where necessary
    if (int(userInput) > 99 and int(userInput)%100 !=
0):
        numText = numText + ' and'

    #Printing the tens
    if (tens == '1'):
        numText = numText + teensMapping[tens+units]
    elif (tens == '0'):
        numText = numText + unitsMapping[units]
    else:
        numText = numText + tensMapping[tens] +
unitsMapping[units]

    #Returning the resulting string
    return numText

# Getting user's input
userInput = input('Enter an integer smaller than
1000: ')

while True:
    try:
        userNum = int(userInput)
        if userNum > 999:
```

```
            userInput = input('Number is too big.
Enter an integer smaller than 1000: ')
        else:
            break
    except ValueError:
        userInput = input('You did not enter an
integer. Enter an integer smaller than 1000: ')

# Calling the printText() function
print(printText(userInput).strip())
```

### *Run Through*

In the code above, we start by defining a function called
`printText()` that has one parameter - `userInput`.

Within this function, we initialize three dictionaries:
`unitsMapping`, `tensMapping` and `teensMapping`.

The `unitsMapping` dictionary maps digits to their English
equivalents. For instance, `'3'` is mapped to `' Three'`. The only
exception is `'0'`, which is mapped to an empty string. A space is
added before the English spelling of each digit as we always add a
space to separate words in our English sentences.

Next, let's look at the `tensMapping` dictionary. This dictionary
maps the tens digits (except when the tens digit is 0 or 1) to their
English spelling.

For instance, if the number is 24, the tens digit is 2.

The `tensMapping` dictionary maps the string `'2'` to `' Twenty'`.

Finally, the last dictionary is the `teensMapping` dictionary. This
dictionary maps numbers between 10 to 19 (inclusive) to their
English equivalents (with space added).

After we finish creating the dictionaries, we use the `len()`
function to get the length of `userInput`. This length will tell us

whether `userInput` is a one digit, two digits or three digits number.

We also initialize a variable called `numText` as an empty string. `numText` will be used to store the English spelling of our number.

Next, we use three inline `if` statements to extract the digits in `userInput`.

Note that `userInput` is a string. In Python, we can treat strings as lists of characters when assessing them.

For instance, if `userInput = '327'`, we can access the individual characters in `userInput` as follows:

```
userInput[0] = '3'
userInput[1] = '2'
userInput[2] = '7'
```

As `numLength` equals 3 in the example above,

```
userInput[numLength - 1] = userInput[2] = '7'
```

In other words, `userInput[numLength - 1]` gives us the units digit.

Similarly, `userInput[numLength - 2]` gives us the tens digit and `userInput[numLength - 3]` gives us the hundreds digit.

After extracting the digits, we are ready to use the dictionaries to map them to their respective English spellings.

The mapping for the digit in the hundreds place is quite straightforward.

The `'3'` in `'327'` is mapped to `' Three'` and concatenated with `' Hundred'` to give us `' Three Hundred'`.

Next, we determine if we need to add the string ' and' to numText. We need to do that if the number is greater than 99 and not a multiple of 100 (userInput%100 != 0).

For instance, if the number is 482, we need to add ' and' as the number is read as "Four Hundred **and** Eighty Two".

On the other hand, if the number is 82, we do not need ' and' as the number is read as "Eighty Two". Similarly, if the number is 300, we do not need ' and' as it'll just be "Three Hundred".

After deciding if we need to add ' and', we move on to map the digits in the tens and units places. This is more tricky.

If the digit in the tens place is '1' (e.g. '315'), we need to concatenate the tens digit with the units digit (tens + units) to get '15' and use the teensMapping dictionary to get the English spelling (teensMapping[tens+units]).

We then concatenate this with numText (which currently has the English spelling of the hundreds digit) and assign it back to numText.

On the other hand, if the digit in the tens place is '0' (e.g. '305'), we only need to map the units digit (unitsMapping[units]) and concatenate it with numText.

Last but not least, if the tens digit is not '0' or '1', we need to map the tens digit and the units digit using the tensMapping and unitsMapping dictionaries separately and concatenate them with numText.

With that, the function is almost complete, we simply need to return the value of numText.

Now we are ready to call the function and print out the result.

We first prompt the user to enter an integer smaller than one thousand.

We then use a `while True` loop to try casting the user's input into an integer.

A `while True` loop is basically a loop that runs indefinitely. This is because writing `while True` is equivalent to writing something like `while 1==1`. Since 1 always equals 1, the `while` condition will never evaluate to `False`. Hence, the loop will run indefinitely.

If we are unable to cast the user's input into an integer, the `except ValueError` block will be executed and the user will be prompted to enter an integer again. This is done repeatedly until we get an integer.

Once we get an integer, the `try` block checks if the integer is greater than 999. If it is, we prompt the user to enter an integer again. If it is not, we have gotten a valid input and can exit the `while True` loop. To exit the loop, we use the `break` statement.

Once we break out of the `while True` loop, we simply call the `printText()` function.

However, as the string returned by the `printText()` function (`printText(userInput)`) has a space before the first word, we need to use the built-in string method `strip()` to strip this space first (`printText(userInput).strip()`).

Once that is done, we pass the result to the `print()` function to print it out.

Clear? Try running the code yourself to see how it works before moving on to Part 2.

### Spelling out Numbers Part 2

In Part 1 of this project, we learned to spell numbers that are smaller than 1000.

In this second part, we are going to spell numbers up to 999,999 (i.e. any integer smaller than 1,000,000).

Try modifying your solution for Part 1 to allow the program to spell up to 999,999. For instance, if the user keys in 123456, the program should display

*One Hundred and Twenty Three Thousand Four Hundred and Fifty Six*

### Suggested Solution

In the solution presented below, we'll modify our program in Part 1 using a concept known as recursion. This allows us to solve the new problem by adding only a few more lines of code to the previous solution.

Before we present our solution, let's look at what recursion means.

Simply stated, recursion refers to a function calling itself during its execution. Let's look at an example.

```
1 def factorial(n):
2    if (n == 1):
3        return 1
4    else:
5        return n*factorial(n-1)
```

This example shows a function that is used to calculate the factorial of a number (line numbers are not part of the code and are added for reference purpose only).

Recall that we wrote a function to calculate factorial in Chapter 6

Question 26? This is an alternative and much shorter method to achieve the same result.

You can see that this function is calling itself on line 5 with the argument `n-1`.

Let's look at a concrete example of how this works. Suppose we want to find the value of 4!.

To do that, we call the `factorial()` function as follows:

```
result = factorial(4)
```

Here, we pass in `4` as the argument.

As 4 does not equal 1, the function skips lines 2 and 3 and goes on to execute lines 4 and 5.

When it reaches line 5, it has to return `4*factorial(3)`.

In other words, it has to execute the `factorial()` function again, with `3` as the argument this time.

When it does that (i.e. when it evaluates `factorial(3)`), the function skips lines 2 and 3 again (as 3 does not equal 1) and goes on to execute lines 4 and 5.

When it reaches line 5, it has to return `3*factorial(2)`. This means that it has to execute the `factorial()` function yet again, with `2` as the argument this time.

This keeps repeating as shown in the manner below:

```
factorial(4)
= 4*factorial(3)
= 4*3*factorial(2)
= 4*3*2*factorial(1)
```

When it finally reaches `4*3*2*factorial(1)`, something

different happens. As the argument to the `factorial()` function is now 1, the function no longer executes line 5.

In other words, it stops calling itself. Instead, it executes lines 2 and 3 and returns the number 1.

Hence, `4*3*2*factorial(1)` becomes `4*3*2*1`, which is the answer that we want.

As you can see, a recursive function will keep calling itself until a certain condition is met. In our example, the condition is when the argument is 1 (`n == 1`). This is known as the base case of the function. A base case is a case that ends the recursion.

Clear? Good!

Now that we understand recursion, let's go back to our project.

Let's analyze how we spell a number greater than 999. Suppose we want to spell 123456.

We spell it as "One Hundred and Twenty Three Thousand Four Hundred and Fifty Six".

Notice that the first three digits (123) can be spelled using the `printText()` function we wrote in Part 1?

This makes it a perfect case for us to use recursion.

We can call the `printText()` function within the `printText()` function itself to help us spell the digits in the thousands place.

Let's look at how we implement this.

We need to make some modifications to the previous `printText()` function.

Replace the comment block

```
'''
This comment block is to be replaced
with code in Part 2
Leave it as it is now
'''
```

in the `printText()` function with the code below:

```
thousands = userInput[:numLength - 3] if
numLength > 3 else '0'

#Printing the thousands
if (thousands != '0'):
    numText = printText(thousands) + ' Thousand'
```

Here, we first use a slice (`[:numLength - 3]`) to get the digits in the thousands place.

Suppose the number is `'123456'`. The slice `[:numLength - 3]` becomes `[ :3]` as `numLength` equals 6.

This gives us the 1$^{st}$, 2$^{nd}$ and 3$^{rd}$ elements of the list. In other words, we get `'123'`, which are the digits in the thousands place.

After we get the digits that we want, we add an `if` statement to execute the recursion.

This `if` statement runs only if we have digits in the thousands place.

In our example, as `thousands = '123'`, the `if` statement will run.

This statement evaluates `printText('123')` and concatenates the result with `' Thousand'`.

With that, the modification to the `printText()` function is complete.

Next, we need to modify the `while True` loop to allow users to input numbers greater than 999.

To do that, change

```
if userNum > 999:
```

to

```
if userNum > 999999:
```

Next, modify the instructions for the `input()` function to prompt users to enter an integer smaller than 1000000 (instead of 1000). We need to modify the instructions thrice as we called the `input()` function thrice.

That's it! You can now try running the function and enter numbers greater than 999. Everything will work as expected.

# Project 2

## Finding nth term of sequences

For this project, we are going to write a program to help us generate formulas for finding the $n^{th}$ term of linear and quadratic number sequences.

## Linear Sequences

A linear sequence is one where the difference between successive terms is always the same. This difference is known as the common difference.

For instance, consider the sequence 3, 7, 11, 15...

The difference between successive terms is constant:
$7 - 3 = 4$
$11 - 7 = 4$
$15 - 11 = 4$

Our job is to generate the formula for getting the $n^{th}$ term of any given linear sequence so that we do not have to keep adding the common difference to get the term that we want.

For instance, for the sequence above, the $n^{th}$ term (denoted by $T_n$) is given by the formula

$T_n = 4n - 1$

To get the $6^{th}$ term (denoted by $T_6$), we simply substitute $n = 6$ into the formula ($T_6 = 4*6 - 1$) to get 23 instead of having to add 4 twice from the $4^{th}$ term ($15 + 4 + 4 = 23$).

So how did we get the formula above?

The $n^{th}$ term of any linear sequence is given by the formula $T_n =$

$an + b$, where n refers to the term number (e.g. for the 5$^{th}$ term, n = 5). We need to figure out the values of a and b, which is different for each linear sequence.

To get the value of a, we subtract the first term from the second term. In other words,

a = Second Term – First Term

To get b, we subtract a from the first term. In other words,

b = First Term – a

I'll skip the math behind these formulas as we do not need to know the math for our coding purpose.

Clear about linear sequences?

### Quadratic Sequences

Good! Let's move on to quadratic sequences.

A quadratic sequence is a sequence where the difference between successive differences is constant.

Confused? Let's consider the sequence 2, 9, 18, 29, 42...

The difference between successive terms is not constant:
9 - 2 = 7
18 - 9 = 9
29 - 18 = 11
42 - 29 = 13

However, the difference between successive differences is constant:
9 - 7 = 2
11 - 9 = 2
13 - 11 = 2

This difference is known as the second difference. A quadratic sequence is one that has a constant second difference.

The formula for the $n^{th}$ term of a quadratic sequence is given by $T_n = an^2 + bn + c$, where n refers to the term number.

The formulas for finding a, b and c are

a = (First term + Third term - 2*Second term)/2
b = (8*Second term - 5*First term - 3*Third term)/2
c = 3*First term - 3*Second term + Third term

Our task for this project is to write a program that does the following:

1. Read from a *.txt* file (*sequences.txt*) and convert each line in the file into a list of integers. If the line cannot be converted, display an appropriate message to inform the user.
2. If the line can be converted, check if the list is a linear or quadratic sequence.
3. If it is either a linear or quadratic sequence, derive the formula for the $n^{th}$ term and print out the formula.
4. If it is not a linear or quadratic sequence, display an appropriate message to inform the user.

Clear?

The *sequences.txt* file contains the following content:

1, 3, 5, 7
1, 3, 6, 10
1, a, c, d
1, 4
5, 8, 1.2, 4.1
2, 9, 18, 29, 42
3, 6, 8, 10, 12

You can do it using any approach you like.

The suggested solution below uses object oriented programming to illustrate how to use classes in our programs. It'll also demonstrate how to use abstract methods in our classes. Note that the code uses Python 3.4 and above. Hence, it will not work properly if you try to run it on a version older than Python 3.4.

### *Suggested Solution*

sequencesolver.py

```python
from abc import ABC, abstractmethod

class Sequence(ABC):
    def __init__(self):
        self._numberList = []

    def __str__(self):
        return '\nSequence = %s' %(self._numberList)

    @abstractmethod
    def findFormula(self):
        pass

    @property
    def numberList(self):
        return self._numberList

    @numberList.setter
    def numberList(self, value):
        if all(isinstance(x, int) for x in value):
            self._numberList = value
        else:
            print('\n%s is not a linear/quadratic
sequence'%(value))

class Quadratic(Sequence):
    def __init__(self):
        super().__init__()

    def __str__(self):
```

```python
        return super().__str__() + '\nThis is a
quadratic sequence'

    def findFormula(self):
        a = (self.numberList[0] + self.numberList[2]
- 2*self.numberList[1])/2
        b = (8*self.numberList[1] -
5*self.numberList[0] - 3*self.numberList[2])/2
        c = 3*self.numberList[0] -
3*self.numberList[1] + self.numberList[2]
        return ('T(n) = %sn^2 + %sn + %s' %(a, b,
c)).replace('+ -', '- ')

class Linear(Sequence):
    def __init__(self):
        super().__init__()

    def __str__(self):
        return super().__str__() + '\nThis is a
linear sequence'

    def findFormula(self):
        a = (self.numberList[1] - self.numberList[0])
        b = (self.numberList[0] - a)
        return ('T(n) = %sn + %s' %(a, b)).replace('+
-', '- ')
```

## main.py

```python
import sequencesolver

def getList(sequence):
    try:
        list1 = sequence.split(',')
        sequenceList = list(map(int, list1))
        return sequenceList
    except:
        return -1

def isQuad(numberList):
    if len(numberList)>=4:
        diff = numberList[2]-
2*numberList[1]+numberList[0]
        for i in range(1, len(numberList)-2):
            if (numberList[i+2]-
```

```
              2*numberList[i+1]+numberList[i] != diff):
                        return False
            return True
        else:
            return False

def isLinear(numberList):
    if len(numberList)>=3:
        diff = numberList[1]-numberList[0]
        for i in range(1, len(numberList)-1):
            if (numberList[i+1]-numberList[i] !=
diff):
                        return False
            return True
        else:
            return False

quad = sequencesolver.Quadratic()
linear = sequencesolver.Linear()

f = open ('sequences.txt', 'r')

for line in f:
    myList = getList(line)
    if (myList == -1):
        print('\n[%s] is not a linear/quadratic
sequence' %(line.strip()))
    else:
        if isLinear(myList):
            linear.numberList = myList
            print(linear)
            print(linear.findFormula())
        elif isQuad(myList):
            quad.numberList = myList
            print(quad)
            print(quad.findFormula())
        else:
            print('\n[%s] is not a linear/quadratic
sequence' %(line.strip()))

f.close()
```

## *Run Through*

The *sequencesolver.py* file starts by importing ABC and

`abstractmethod` from the `abc` module.

`abc` stands for "abstract base classes" and is a built-in module that provides the infrastructure for defining abstract classes in Python.

Don't worry about what abstract classes are at the moment. We'll come back to them very soon.

After importing the module, we declare a class called `Sequence` that inherits from the `ABC` class. The `ABC` class is included in the `abc` module and is used to create an abstract class.

So what is an abstract class?

Simply put, an abstract class is a parent class that contains an abstract method. An abstract method is a method that has no body and must be implemented in the derived class. Abstract classes cannot be instantiated.

Confused? Let's start with a simple example of an abstract class.

Suppose we have a class called `Pets` and intend to derive three subclasses – `Dogs`, `Cats` and `Rabbits` – from this class.

We want all three subclasses to have a method for displaying the vaccination requirements of the pet. How can we enforce that?

We can declare an abstract method called `displayVaccination()` in the parent class (`Pets`).

When we do that, we are indicating that we want any subclass derived from the `Pets` class to implement this method. If the subclass does not implement the method, it cannot be instantiated.

Clear?

Note that we do not need to implement the abstract method in the parent class (Pets) itself. This makes sense as "pets" is an abstract concept and different types of pets have different vaccination requirements. Hence, we cannot display the requirements of a "pet" per se.

In order to indicate that a parent class is an abstract class, it has to inherit the ABC class. In our code, the Sequence class inherits the ABC class.

It has one abstract method called findFormula(). To indicate that findFormula() is an abstract method, we have to add the @abstractmethod decorator before it.

Within the method, we did not add any code to it except for the pass statement. This statement is kind of like a dummy statement. It does nothing other than to satisfy a syntax requirement.

This is because Python expects us to add an indented block after we declare a method. If we do not do that, Python will give us an error that says "expected an indented block".

To prevent that, we just have to add the pass statement.

Alternatively, we can also add an indented comment as shown below:

```
@abstractmethod
def findFormula(self):
    'Implement in subclasses'
```

Besides declaring the findFormula() method, we also coded the __init__ and __str__ methods for the Sequence class.

The __init__ method initializes the instance variable _numberList to an empty list and the __str__ method returns a string representation of the class.

Next, we added a property for the instance variable _numberList.

The setter method uses the `all()` function to check if `value` is a list of integers.

The argument

```
isinstance(x, int) for x in value
```

loops through `value` (using `for x in value`) and uses the built-in Python function `isinstance()` to check if `x` is an integer.

We pass this argument to the `all()` function.

The `all()` function is another built-in Python function that returns `True` if `isinstance()` returns `True` for <u>all</u> values of `x`.

This is the easiest way to check if all elements in a list are integers.

Alternatively, we can loop through and check the list ourselves using the code below:

```
allIntegers = True

for x in value:
    if (isinstance(x, int) == False):
        allIntegers = False
        break

if (allIntegers):
    #Do something
```

This achieves the same result but is a longer way to do it.

After we verify that all elements in `value` are integers, we assign `value` to the instance variable `_numberList` using the statement

```
self._numberList = value
```

On the other hand, if `value` is not a list of integers, we print a message to notify the user that the input is not a sequence.

With that, our `Sequence` class is complete.

Next, we declare two subclasses – `Linear` and `Quadratic` – that derive from the `Sequence` class. These two subclasses implement the `findFormula()` method according to the formulas given in the project description above.

Once that is done, the *sequencesolver.py* file is complete.

Now we need to create another file called *main.py* and import the three classes (`Sequence`, `Linear` and `Quadratic`) using the statement
```
import sequencesolver
```

We then declare three functions – `getList()`, `isQuad()` and `isLinear()`.

The `getList()` function has one parameter – `sequence`.

Inside the function, we use a `try-except` statement to perform the following tasks.

First, we use the built-in Python method `split()` to split `sequence` into a list of substrings, using `', '` as a delimiter. We assign the resulting list to `list1`.

Next, we use the `map()` function to convert `list1` (which is a list of strings) into a list of integers.

The `map()` function is a built-in Python function that applies a function to all the elements of an iterable (such as a list). It accepts the names of the function and the iterable as arguments and returns the result as a map object.

Here, we use the `map()` function (`map(int, list1)`)) to apply the `int()` function to all elements in `list1`.

As the `map()` function returns a map object, we use the built-in `list()` function to convert it into a list.

As you can see, the `map()` function is a convenient way to cast all the elements of a list into integers.

Alternatively, if we do not use the `map()` function, we can also do it as follows:

```
sequenceList = []
for x in list1:
    sequenceList.append(int(x))
```

This is a slightly longer way to achieve the same result.

After we get the input as a list of integers, we return the list. If any of the steps above fails, our `try` block generates an error and we return -1 as the result. With that, the `getList()` function is complete.

The next function is the `isQuad()` function. This function has one parameter `numberList` and checks if `numberList` contains a quadratic sequence.

In order to do that, let's consider the following quadratic sequence: 2, 9, 18, 29, 42...

A sequence is quadratic if the second difference is constant.

In other words, we need to check the second differences for all the numbers in the sequence.

For the first three numbers in the sequence above, we can calculate the second difference as follows:

$9 - 2 = 7$
$18 - 9 = 9$

Second Difference = 9 − 7 = 2

For the 2nd to 4th number, we calculate it as follows:
18 − 9 = 9
29 − 18 = 11
Second Difference = 11 − 9 = 2

From these two examples, we can derive a formula for getting all the second differences in the sequence.

Suppose we have a list called `num`. We can get the 1$^{st}$ second difference by subtracting

```
num[1] - num[0]
```

from

```
num[2] - num[1]
```

In other words,

The 1$^{st}$ second difference
```
= (num[2] - num[1]) - (num[1] - num[0])
= num[2] - 2*num[1] + num[0]
```

For any element at index `i`, we can generalize the equation as:

Second difference
```
= num[i+2] - 2*num[i+1] + num[i]
```

Let's consider the `isQuad()` function shown below (line numbers are added for reference):

```
1 def isQuad(numberList):

2    if len(numberList)>=4:

3        diff = numberList[2]-2*numberList[1] +
numberList[0]
```

```
4          for i in range(1, len(numberList)-2):

5               if (numberList[i+2] - 2*numberList[i+1]
+ numberList[i] != diff):

6                   return False

7          return True

8      else:
9          return False
```

In our `isQuad()` function, we first check if `numberList` has at least 4 elements (line 2). Without 4 elements, we will not be able to determine if the second difference is constant.

If `numberList` has less than 4 elements, we return `False` (lines 8 and 9). Else, we do the following (lines 3 to 7):

We first use the first three elements to get the 1st second difference and assign this to a variable called `diff` (line 3).

Next, we loop through the list (line 4) to check if any of the subsequent second differences differ from `diff` (line 5).

If any of them does, the sequence is not a quadratic sequence and we return `False` (line 6).

After looping through the entire list, if we do not find any second difference that differs from `diff`, we return `True` (line 7).

With that, the `isQuad()` function is complete and we move on to the `isLinear()` function.

The `isLinear()` function is much easier to code because the difference can be calculated by subtracting any number from the next number in the sequence.

For instance, if the sequence is 4, 7, 10, 13...

We calculate the difference by subtracting 4 from 7 (7 - 4 = 3) or 7 from 10 or 10 from 13.

Other than that, the `isLinear()` function follows the same logic as the `isQuad()` function.

Once we finish coding the three functions, we can start generating our formulas.

We first instantiate a `Quadratic` object called `quad` and a `Linear` object called `linear`.

Next, we open the *sequences.txt* file and loop through it line by line. Each line is read in as a string.

We then use the `getList()` function to convert the string into a list of integers.

If we are unable to convert the string into a list of integers (`myList == -1`), we inform the user that the string is not a sequence.

Else, we use the `isLinear()` and `isQuad()` functions to check if `myList` is a linear or quadratic sequence.

If it is a linear sequence, we assign `myList` to the `numberList` variable of `linear` and use the `print()` function to print a string representation of the instance.

Next, we use the instance to call the `findFormula()` method. This gives us the n$^{\text{th}}$ term formula as a string. We pass the resulting string to the `print()` function to print the formula.

On the other hand, if `myList` is a quadratic sequence, we do the same as above using the `Quadratic` object `quad`.

Finally, if `myList` is neither linear nor quadratic, we inform the user.

With that, the program is almost done. Once we finish looping through the file, we simply close it using the `close()` function.

If you run the program, you'll get the following output:

*Sequence = [1, 3, 5, 7]*
*This is a linear sequence*
*T(n) = 2n - 1*

*Sequence = [1, 3, 6, 10]*
*This is a quadratic sequence*
*T(n) = 0.5n^2 + 0.5n + 0*

*[1, a, c, d] is not a linear/quadratic sequence*

*[1, 4] is not a linear/quadratic sequence*

*[5, 8, 1.2, 4.1] is not a linear/quadratic sequence*

*Sequence = [2, 9, 18, 29, 42]*
*This is a quadratic sequence*
*T(n) = 1.0n^2 + 4.0n - 3*

*[3, 6, 8, 10, 12] is not a linear/quadratic sequence*

Manufactured by Amazon.ca
Bolton, ON